How to Make God Happy

A Fresh and Balanced Look at Faith

Sal DiMare

How to Make God Happy
© 2013 by Sal DiMare

To my wife, Rhonda, whose devotion is constant and for whose love I am grateful. You are God's gift to me and a true partner in ministry.

To my three sons—Andrew, Alex, and Abraham—I can't imagine how any father could be more proud of his children. Your dedication to God and enthusiasm for His Kingdom is inspiring

Contents

Introduction

I don't view God as inherently unhappy. There are obviously some things that make Him not only unhappy but even angry. Even so, I believe He is indeed happy. You may have picked up this book and thought, *I would like to make God happy.* The answer is easier than you might think. Others may look at this and say something like, "It is impossible to have any effect on God whatsoever." I know what people mean when they say a thing like that, but, for some reason, the infinite God of the universe has taken a great interest in the humans He created. While we can't change God's nature in any way, we can do things that either please Him or displease Him.

Before I go any further, I want to make something very clear for those of us who are believers. God is pleased with us. He is happy with each of us as a person. By the way, it is not because of anything we did or didn't do. He is pleased with us because we had faith in His Son for salvation, and He will never be displeased with who we are. It would be naïve, however, to link His pleasure with us to everything we do. God can't be happy with some of the things we do because sometimes we sin, and this clearly does not please God. So, as we continue to explore this idea of making God happy, please don't ever—not for one moment—question His pleasure with us as individuals. This book is about pleasing God with what we do and how we face life.

The entirety of what I want to say can be summed up in one sentence from one verse in the book of Hebrews:

"Without faith it is impossible to please God."
(Hebrews 11:6)

The word "please" means to cause to feel happy and satisfied. So, it is in fact possible to make God happy. In reality, if we take this verse at face value, there is only *one thing* that will make Him happy and please Him. It is faith! Wuest translates this phrase, "But without faith it is impossible to please Him at all."[1] "At all!" It is the only thing human beings can do to please God. That being said, we ought to take faith very seriously.

In writing a book on faith I hesitate because I do not feel that I am as strong in my faith as I ought to be. I am growing in my faith, but I ask myself, "Who am I to write a book about this great subject?" I wish I had more wonderful faith stories to share to inspire people, but I am still on a journey in this area. I take solace in a couple of things: First, a person doesn't necessarily have to be the best player to be a good coach. I believe God has given me insight and the ability to explain things so others might excel. Second, Paul the apostle said, "Not that I have already obtained all this, or have already arrived at my goal, but I press on to take hold of that for which Christ Jesus took hold of me" (Philippians 3:12). The great apostle Paul said, in essence, "I haven't got this all figured out yet, but I am still working on it." If he could say that in the Bible then I guess I can say it in a book.

If faith, and faith alone, pleases God or makes Him happy then we owe it to ourselves to take inventory in every area to see if we are living in and by faith. A quick examination of the chapter titles of this book will reveal that an attempt has been made to cover what, for most part, are the main areas of concern in life. By becoming people of faith in these areas, we not only please God but we begin to live the kind of life that God intended us to live.

We hear many people say, "When I stand before the Lord,

all I want to hear Him say to me is, 'Well done, good and faithful servant.'" That phrase is found in the story of the talents in Matthew's Gospel (Matthew 25:14–30). It is spoken twice—once to each of the servants who wisely and faithfully used what the master had given them. In the story, the master is God and we are the servants. The talents were units of money, but in the big scheme of things they represent our lives—what we have been given to work with. The expectation of the Master is that His servants will take the life we have been given and use it well so that when it is over we can stand before God and hear those words we long to hear from Him, "Well done." The interpretation of this parable comes to us from the context in Matthew 25. Jesus is speaking about the end times and what will happen when this life is over.

> "Well done, good and faithful servant! You have been faithful with a few things; I will put you in charge of many things. Come and share your master's happiness!" (Matthew 25:21)

He says, "Well done, *good* and faithful servant!" (emphasis mine). The truth is, apart from the forgiveness of sins through believing in Christ and His death, burial, and resurrection, we cannot be good. In fact, the Bible says point-blank, "No one is good—except God alone" (Luke 18:19). So, the only way we can appear before God and hear Him say to us that we are "good" is if His goodness has been somehow given to us or, perhaps better said, if God lives inside us then we would be considered good. Again, it is not because of our own goodness but because His goodness has been credited to us. When God says to us someday, "Well done, good . . .," He will be speaking to the fact that good is in us because of what *He* did for us. The bottom line: Good is God's part.

He says, "Well done, good and *faithful* servant!" (emphasis mine). This part is on us. Yes, of course, God is faithful and

11

somehow His faithfulness will work through us, but it really is up to us to *be faithful* and to *show faithfulness* in this life. As I said, that is the point of this parable. Those who were faithful were given more and welcomed. The servant who hid what he was given had it taken from him and he was banished from the presence of the master. The bottom line: Faith is our part.

Finally, He says, "Come and share your master's happiness!" The book you are reading is titled *How to Make God Happy*. It is an absurd title because, as we see, God is already happy. In fact, happiness is a state of being for God. He, in Himself, is happy. (Again, this does not mean that God cannot be sad or angry with certain things. The amazing thing about God is He can do more than one thing at the same time. In fact, He can be more than one thing at the same time. This helps us to, in some small way, understand the Trinity and how Jesus Christ could be fully God and fully man at the same time.) So, please, let's not have an image in our minds of a grumpy, surly God but of a God who will some day welcome us into His happiness.

This book is about how we can please God by doing our part: being faithful and faith-filled. Let's journey together—not through a book—but through a day-by-day exercise we know pleases God. Let's make God happy!

Chapter One
Mustard-Tree Faith

I am troubled . . . (That is not a good way to start a book. Let me try again.)

I am disturbed . . . (No, that's worse. It makes it sound like I need a psychiatric evaluation. One more try . . .)

I am frustrated! I can't help it. I have been a pastor for nearly thirty years, and I am bothered about something. When I read the Bible, specifically the Gospels and the Book of Acts, I keep reading about incredible miracles. To be honest, I have not seen very many things in my life or ministry that I would consider bona fide miracles, and the fact is I really need to. Not just for myself, but for others. It seems to be a really important part of the ministry of Jesus—not only for the Lord but for the disciples as well.

I see the importance of miracles in the New Testament narrative as twofold. First, there is the need being met for the one who receives the miracle. A woman receives her son back from the dead. A man who had never walked is now able to walk and carry his own mat. Thousands of hungry people are fed when a boy shares what is ostensibly a Filet-O-Fish® sandwich. Another man who, moments ago, was begging is now walking, leaping, and praising God throughout the temple. I don't know about you, but if I am one of those people I am thrilled at the miracle that has been performed. The second benefit is that miracles seem to attract people to hear the gospel and receive salvation. What could be more important than salvation? Jesus Himself said, "For what will it profit a man if he gains the whole world, and loses his own soul?" (Mark 8:36 NKJV).

I don't know about you, but miracles sound great to me, and I am frustrated that I don't see more. In fact, I don't just feel that it would be nice; I believe the Lord expects us to be doing miracles. He said, "Very truly I tell you, whoever believes in me will do the works I have been doing, and they will do even greater things than these, because I am going to the Father" (John 14:12).

Please look at the verse above and focus on the word "faith." Now go back a few words and notice the word "anyone." Would you be willing to stop reading for a moment and not just think about this but pray a simple prayer and say something like: "Lord, You said if I had faith in You I could do the things You did. Please help me to be obedient to Your command here."

When we read that anyone with faith in Christ will do what He did and when we read that it is impossible to please God without faith, we may begin to wonder if we have enough faith. I mean how much faith does it take to do something miraculous? Do I have any faith at all for doing the works of Christ? The Bible says that God gives every person a measure of faith and that even faith as a mustard seed is enough to move a mountain.

Some may have read that last sentence and thought I misquoted Jesus's words found in Matthew 17:20. I have heard many preachers preach about mountain-moving faith and say the words, "If you have faith as *small* as a mustard seed . . ." In fact, several translations use the word small.

I want to show you something remarkable. In the original Greek language this sentence looks like this:

εαν   εχητε   πιστιν ως   κοκκον   σιναπεως
If – you have – faith – as – a grain – (of) mustard (seed)

There are two words for small in the Greek language:
μικρός - *micros* – "little, small" (of age, quantity, size, space)
ὀλίγος - *oligos* – "little, small" (of amount, number, time)

Notice that neither of these words is actually used in the sentence. Why is the word "small" inserted in some English translations? Apparently some of those translating the text thought it was implied. But if we read it as it was actually spoken by Jesus we get a very different and important meaning. Jesus is literally saying, "If you have faith *as* a mustard seed."

What is the difference? If we look at something Jesus said in Matthew 13, we get a better understanding.

> "He told them another parable: 'The kingdom of heaven is like a mustard seed, which a man took and planted in his field. Though it is the smallest of all your seeds, yet when it grows, it is the largest of garden plants and becomes a tree, so that the birds of the air come and perch in its branches.'" (Matthew 13:31–32)

Are you starting to see the difference and significance of this? The overarching point of the mustard seed is that *it grows*.

Now let me clear something up here. Jesus said a seed. Why didn't He say faith as small as a grain of sand or small pebble? Because you can't plant a pebble in the ground, water it, and fertilize it, and come back in a few weeks and say, "Oooooh, look, a pebble tree!" I guarantee you that the pebble will be the same size it was when you planted it. A seed on the other hand, when properly nurtured, will grow and grow and grow. With that in mind, let us examine the verse in the English Standard Version (which in my opinion does a better job with the text) where the mustard seed is mentioned in Matthew.

And when they came to the crowd, a man came

up to him and, kneeling before him, said, "Lord, have mercy on my son, for he is an epileptic and he suffers terribly. For often he falls into the fire, and often into the water. And I brought him to your disciples, and they could not heal him." And Jesus answered, "O faithless and twisted generation, how long am I to be with you? How long am I to bear with you? Bring him here to me." And Jesus rebuked him, and the demon came out of him, and the boy was healed instantly. Then the disciples came to Jesus privately and said, "Why could we not cast it out?" He said to them, "Because of your little faith. For truly, I say to you, if you have faith like a grain of mustard seed, you will say to this mountain, 'Move from here to there,' and it will move, and nothing will be impossible for you." (Matthew 17:14–20 ESV)

I have asked many people about this, and there seems to be a pattern. For most, when we first become believers, prayers seem to rise to God's throne and be answered more easily and many times quickly. As new believers we often feel that God is very close and we may sense an excitement in our newfound faith because God is so real—not only in answered prayer, but we seem to see Him at work in even the smallest details of our lives. We read the Bible, and its words leap off the pages as we discover new truths and promises everyday. As time passes, though, we begin to lose that sense of God's closeness. Our prayers seem to stop inches above our heads. Our time in the Word becomes a discipline rather than a joy.

My aunt Mary was a woman of faith. She really trusted God and taught me to do the same. One time after an evening church service, we walked out of the building into the dark. She didn't see a step and fell, twisting her ankle badly. We had to help her to the car and get her home because she was unable to put weight on the leg. When we got a better look at it in the light, the ankle was swollen to twice its size and turned at an unnatural angle. To my estimation as a fifteen-year-old, I believed it was broken.

She called to me and said, "Sal, come pray for me." I had only known the Lord for a few months, and I was absolutely convinced that God could do miracles. (I hadn't learned how hard that was yet.) So I prayed for her, and she immediately felt relief. Her ankle became straight and less swollen. She stood up and was able to put weight on it. I would like to tell you that she was completely healed at that moment, but there were a few days of limping to follow. Even so, I was convinced God had done a miracle.

Many years later while doing some construction on our house, I tried to lift a sheet of plywood over my head and toss it up to the second story. Somehow the plywood slipped out of my hands and fell, directly hitting my knee. The pain was excruciating.

My son Andrew, who was six at the time, was playing nearby. When I cried out in pain, he came running and asked if I was okay. All I could say was, "Pray for me, son." He laid his little hand on my knee and prayed a simple, faith-filled prayer. Immediately the pain disappeared. I remembered my aunt having me pray for her and now began to see the principle of having children and young believers pray for miracles because their faith seems to be stronger than that of adults.

As we get older in our relationship with God, it seems that we too easily replace faith with doubt. We pray for healing and for needs mostly as an obligation, but we secretly doubt anything will happen because we have prayed so many times and seen little or no results.

Some time ago as I was studying for a sermon, the answer to my dilemma hit me like the proverbial ton of bricks. Small faith is fine for new believers and is indeed capable of moving mountains. But as we mature in our life with God, He expects our faith to grow along with that relationship. He starts out graciously working with us as we are, new in our faith, and many times He gives us what we ask of Him. But, over time, we see the truth that "to whom much is given, much is required." In other words, our faith must grow and keep pace with our relationship with God. This then is the point of the mustard seed. As a new believer, faith even as small as a mustard seed can move a mountain, but as we mature in the Lord our faith must also grow. As mature believers we now need mustard-*tree* faith.

Little Faith

Let me explore this further with you.

The apostle Peter seems to always get a bad rap for sort of bumbling along in his relationship with Jesus. He becomes the brunt of jokes about being the man with the "sandal-shaped mouth." He also seems to be the person who leaps before he looks.

One evening Jesus sent His disciples across the Sea of Galilee then He went up on a mountainside to pray. The Sea of Galilee is only about seven miles wide at the widest point, so it is possible as the storm arose that Jesus could see from His vantage point that His disciples were not making much progress.

I like to think about the conversations Jesus may have had with His Father at times like these. I can't help but wonder if in prayer that evening they might have had a good laugh together as Jesus thought about the reactions the disciples were going to have as He walked on the water near them.

Later that evening, Jesus began the trek. After walking on water halfway across the lake, it is past 3:00 a.m. He has reached the point where the weary and likely very wet disciples are still straining to make headway.

Here's a good question: Why were the disciples going to the other side of the lake? When the wind came up against them, why didn't they just turn around and go back? I can only think of one answer. They were obeying Jesus. They were doing exactly what Jesus told them to do, even though the circumstances were against them. Shame on us for many times letting circumstances make us give up on obeying the Lord. I have talked to many people who have felt a call to ministry, but something went wrong so they gave up on it. If Jesus told you to do it, then do it.

In all this, I love the determination of the disciples who have been rowing and struggling to do what they were told, in spite of the circumstances. God help us all to have that kind of determination. If they had given up and gone back, the story would have ended there. Unknown to them, Jesus had almost reached the boat.

One time I read about a mother who was watching her four-year-old son playing outside in a small, plastic pool half-filled with water. He was happily walking back and forth across the pool, making big splashes. Suddenly, the little boy stopped, stepped out of the pool, and began to scoop water out of the pool with a pail. "Why are you pouring the water out, dear?" asked the mother.

"Because my teacher said Jesus walked on water, and this water doesn't work," he replied.

Well, that day on the Sea of Galilee the water worked! Now, in the dark and through the wind-whipped rain, the disciples saw someone walking on the water near them. They were terrified, but He spoke and assured them that He was not a ghost.

Who was the first person to speak up in this situation? None other than Peter. I am sure the other disciples were not surprised to hear his voice above the sound of the wind and the waves. But what Peter *said* must have been a complete shock. He shouted, "Lord, if it's you, tell me to come to you on the water" (Matthew 14:28).

Who thinks like that? Who else would have the nerve to make such a request? Again, (because I have a view of a happy God) I like to imagine a large smile on the face of Jesus as He says, "Come."

The next sentence in our Bibles ought to amaze us: "Then Peter got down out of the boat, walked on the water and came toward Jesus" (Matthew 14:29).

Forget for a moment what you know about the rest of the story. Look again at that sentence. Break it down to a simple statement. Peter walked on the water. Hello? Are we getting this? Bumbling, stumbling Peter put one foot out of the boat and found that water felt like solid ground. Then he pulled his other foot over the gunwale and found traction there as well. Turning toward Jesus and looking right at Him, Peter began to put one foot in front of the other and walked toward the Lord.

If ever there was an illustration of great faith, this is it. "Faith is the substance . . ." Liquid becomes substantive under the pressure of each step. I have met people of great faith in my life, but I have never met anyone who has done what Peter did here. It is astounding. I wish for Peter's sake that this was the end of the story, but it is not.

You know how it goes. Peter took his eyes off the Lord and began to notice the waves and saw the effects of the wind slicing the tops off the waves and turning them into spray. Rather than keeping his attention on the object of his faith, he, like all of us, began to look at the circumstances and lost footing. Instead of solid substance, the water began to resume its natural properties, and, in a moment, Peter went from standing to sinking. Jesus reached out for him and helped him back to his feet, then they both walked on water back to the boat. Don't miss that! Peter walked on water *twice*: first, by keeping his eyes on the Lord, and, *second*, by being held by the Lord as they both went to the boat. (I'm sure there is a great sermon there somewhere.)

As Jesus reached out and helped hold Peter up, we would expect that Jesus would say, "Great job, Peter! You walked on water!" We would normally think that the Lord would commend him for having the guts to try and for actually making some progress in his faith. We could almost imagine

Jesus saying to Peter, "I am so proud of you." We might envision the Lord giving Peter a poke in the ribs with His elbow and saying, "I didn't see any of the other guys even try. But you did, and you actually *walked on water.*"

My made-up scenario sounds reasonable to me, and I guess that is what I would expect from the Lord because, remember, I believe God to be intrinsically happy. But when we keep reading the Gospel account, we find that Jesus's reaction was not at all what we thought it should be. He does not seem pleased at all. Instead of affirmation we read disappointment. "You of little faith," He said, "why did you doubt?" (Matthew 14:31). We might even extrapolate that Jesus is *unhappy* with Peter.

Little faith!? Are you kidding me? In all honesty, the Lord's response seems a bit over the top to me. I was expecting an, "Atta boy," but what Peter got was correction. I feel Jesus is being hard on Peter, but then I remember the mustard seed. You see, when Peter first began to follow the Lord, faith as small as a mustard seed was all he needed. But, now, Peter has been a disciple for some time, and clearly the Lord's hope is that Peter's faith should have grown more by this point. Jesus expects that Peter should have been able to keep focused and stay on top of the water. Little faith just won't do anymore. By this time Peter's faith should have increased. It is obvious that Jesus's expectation was for Peter to have stayed above the waves.

I have known the Lord for over forty years, and I am ashamed to say that my faith is way too small for how long I have walked with Him. Forgive me if this seems indelicate, but many of us have become quadriplegics in our faith. Some of us have known the Lord for ten, twenty, thirty, or forty years, and our faith is still as small as it was when we started. We are too paralyzed to take the leaps of faith we ought to be taking by this time.

This will not do! We need to grow up in our faith! For a believer who has known the Lord for several years, mustard-seed-*size* faith will no longer suffice. That seed should have sprouted and grown to be a tree large enough for the birds of the air to land in. We need mustard-*tree* faith! In our effort to do the things that Jesus did and live a life pleasing to God, we see clearly that small faith won't do.

Mega Faith

We have been looking at "little" faith in the previous story, but now let us look at "great" faith. There are two individuals in the Gospels whom Jesus says had great faith. Interestingly, it was to none of His disciples He said this and neither of them were Jews.

The first was the Canaanite woman whose daughter suffered from demon possession. Upon first glance, we are troubled at Jesus's response when this poor woman asked Him for help. Initially, He completely ignored her even though she cried out. After she got through to Him and made her request, He refused to help and stated that His mission (while here on earth) was to the Jews. And then, in what almost seems to be an ethnic slur, He said, "It is not right to take the children's bread and toss it to the dogs" (Matthew 15:26).

Let me pause for a moment to address the apparent repulse of this woman by the Lord. Here is a great rule of thumb: Always remember that God is good, and if you ever see a place in the Bible where it *appears* He is not acting good, dig deeper until you find the ultimate good in His motive.

Jesus is not rude and He is not prejudiced. The way he responded to this woman purposefully drew out of her the faith needed to obtain her miracle. Without such faith, I don't believe Jesus would have been able to help her. With a mother's love for her daughter as motivation, she pursued and persisted. She stayed very focused and would not let the wind of being ignored or the waves of perceived insult keep her from receiving her daughter's deliverance. She stepped out of her comfort zone into the "storm." Her response to Jesus's statement about giving bread to dogs was, "Even the dogs eat the crumbs that fall from their master's table" (Matthew 15:27). Her faith buoyed her up. There would be no sinking beneath the waves for her.

In my imagination (once again), I see a broad smile coming to the Savior's face and a joyful tone to His voice as He says to her, "Woman, you have great faith! Your request is granted" (Matthew 15:28). She is told that she has *great faith*. That is what Jesus wanted. He was not reluctant to help; He just needed her to exercise her faith. The Lord was impressed with her, whereas the night before he was unimpressed with Peter, who had not been able to keep his focus and stay on top of the water.

The Greek word for "great" in verse 28 is *megas*. It is where the English prefix "mega" comes from. Jesus tells this woman she has mega-faith! It is the same word that was used by Jesus in Mark 4:32 referring to the branches of the mustard tree.

Wuest translates the passage this way: "It is like a grain of mustard seed, which when it is planted in the earth, is less than all the seeds which are upon the earth; and when it is sown, it grows up and becomes greater than all of the herbs, and puts out great branches, so that the birds of the heaven are able to find shelter under its shadow."[2]

On the surface, having faith that your daughter would be healed sounds easier than having faith to walk on water. I mean we have all heard of healing miracles before. From the time of Abraham and Sarah in Genesis and throughout the Old Testament we have stories of healings. However, the perceived difficulty of the miracle is not the issue at all. Nothing is too difficult for our God. Nothing is impossible for Him. He can do all things!

To God, cancer is no different that a sore throat. *We* are the ones who ascribe levels of difficulty to miracles. We pray rather casually for someone with a cold, but for a person who lies dying of organ failure we get prayer teams together and cry out to God for hours. We go without food trying to get God's attention. We call the pastor, we call the prayer chain, and we call the televangelist and even send an offering to get the prayer cloth he offers. We hear of a church that is experiencing miracles, and we go there hoping their prayers are somehow better than ours. (Do you hear the crunching sound as I am stepping on toes here?)

I just want to go on record that I am not against any of the above efforts, and, in fact, many people have experienced healing through things like these, but I do not believe any miracle will take place without faith. In all honesty, I never see Jesus doing any of these kinds of things. I never even see Jesus actually "praying" for the sick. He seems to only ever just proclaim that the healing has taken place.

The Canaanite woman had "mega-faith," and the next words out of Jesus's mouth were, "Your request is granted." We are told that "her daughter was healed instantly" (Matthew 15:28 ESV). Jesus made a simple proclamation in response to her faith, and it was done. Her daughter was healed.

The second person Jesus declared to have "mega-faith" was the centurion. This familiar story bears some similarity to the first. A Roman centurion came to Jesus and asked for healing for his servant, who was ill at home. Jesus immediately responded that He would go heal the servant. But the centurion, in sincere humility, said he was not worthy to have Christ come into his home. He said Jesus should "just *say the word* (emphasis mine), and my servant will be healed" (Matthew 8:8). He continued, "For I myself am a man under authority, with soldiers under me. I tell this one, 'Go,' and he goes; and that one, 'Come,' and he comes. I say to my servant, 'Do this,' and he does it" (Matthew 8:9). When Jesus heard the faith of this man He was astonished (*thaumazoo* in the Greek). We should be astonished that Jesus was astonished. Although the same form of the word *thaumazoo* is used forty-three times in the New Testament, only twice do we see that Jesus is said to be so impressed by something so that *He* is astonished.

The only other mention of Jesus being astonished had to do with His trip to Nazareth early in His ministry. He was able to heal only a few of the sick people there because of their lack of belief or faith. We read that Jesus "was amazed (*thaumazoo*) at their lack of faith" (Mark 6:6). Consider that Jesus's recorded astonishment was over polar opposites. One group of people had a lack of faith, contrasted with the centurion who had great faith.

What made this man's faith so impressive to Jesus? Taking the story at face value, I believe it was the fact that this man knew that all Jesus had to do was "say the word." His faith was so elevated that he was somehow convinced that proximity was not an issue for Jesus. He understood that Christ had the authority to simply speak and the servant would be healed (more on this subject in chapter 11). Just as Peter said on that stormy night, "Lord, if it is You (or as Wuest translates, 'Since it is you') command me to come to You." Lord, just say the word and I will come. Your word, Lord, is more powerful than nature or any other thing. At Your word I will walk upon the waves with You.

Mega-faith is faith that is convinced, and it is faith that will not give up until the answer comes. Mega-faith is faith *as* a mustard seed. For those who are new in their faith this may seem almost easy, but for those of us who have known the Lord for some time, we are going to have to grow up and dig deeper to begin to see the miracles we need in our lives. What does this kind of faith look like? It looks like stepping out of a boat on a stormy night and staying on top of the waves. In the next several chapters I will address various areas in which we might begin to learn how to exercise our faith in the practical issues of life.

Chapter Two
Faith the Facts

The title of this chapter is not a typo and, no, I do not have a lisp. Faith is perhaps the most important subject in the Bible.

Consider this:
- It is by faith we are saved.
- Faith heals us and makes us well.
- Faith removes obstacles in our lives.
- We are justified and considered righteous by faith.
- God's promises are obtained by faith.
- We gain access to God by faith.
- Because of faith we can approach God with confidence.
- We live by faith.
- Faith is a shield that extinguishes the flaming arrows of the evil one.
- Those who have faith are blessed.
- It is through faith that we inherit what was promised.
- Without faith it is impossible to please God. Or to say it a different way, faith is the only thing that truly pleases God.
- Prayer offered in faith makes the sick person well.
- Faith overcomes the world.
- And in one place Paul goes as far as to say, "The *only thing that counts* is faith expressing itself through love" (Galatians 5:6, emphasis mine).

I don't know of anything else that will do all that! So how important is faith? (For more on the benefits and attributes of faith, see the appendix "Amazing Faith in the New Testament.")

In the Bible when faith is mentioned, there is one person whose name seems to come up more often than anyone else— Abraham. He is considered the "Father of Faith." His story in the Book of Genesis is filled with many examples, but the greatest of those examples is retold in Romans 4. Both Abraham and his wife, Sarah, were too old to have children. Having a child, especially a boy, was of monumental importance to people in the Old Testament— particularly for women.

This is because when Adam and Eve sinned, God told Eve that through her offspring One would come who would reverse the curse: "*He*" would defeat the serpent. The following generations did not know or understand that it would be through a virgin that the Messiah would come. So every woman who was a God-follower wanted to have a male child in the hope that the promise would come through her offspring. And in a sense, all the women whose offspring ended up being in the line of Mary were a part of that. Women like Eve, Sarah, Rebekah, Leah, Ruth, Bathsheba, and many others were literally part of the human line of Christ.

Even though Jesus Christ has already been born of Mary, bearing children remains vitally important. Where would the world be if the mothers of Galileo, DaVinci, Pasteur, Franklin, Lincoln, Martin Luther King Jr., and a host of others had not had children? This is another reason, beyond the tragedy of the loss of human life, that abortion is so destructive. It not only extinguishes life but it extinguishes *potential*. Who knows what great discoveries might have been made by the over 55 million children who have been aborted since 1973 in the United States alone?

For Abraham and Sarah to have a child was extremely important. In fact, when Abraham was seventy-five years old,

God promised him that he would have offspring who would become a great nation (Genesis 12:2). The wonder of Abraham's faith is that after twenty-five years with no children, he didn't give up. He did not receive the promised son until he was one hundred years old. This makes his faith so exemplary.

> Against all hope, Abraham in hope believed and so became the father of many nations, just as it had been said to him, "So shall your offspring be." Without weakening in his faith, he faced the fact that his body was as good as dead—since he was about a hundred years old—and that Sarah's womb was also dead. Yet he did not waver through unbelief regarding the promise of God, but was strengthened in his faith and gave glory to God, being fully persuaded that God had power to do what he had promised. This is why "it was credited to him as righteousness." The words "it was credited to him" were written not for him alone, but also for us, to whom God will credit righteousness—for us who believe in him who raised Jesus our Lord from the dead. He was delivered over to death for our sins and was raised to life for our justification. (Romans 4:18–25)

I want to examine three highlights from this passage regarding Abraham's approach to the facts. We see that he did not weaken, he did not waver, and he was fully persuaded. He did not allow facts to stand in the way. He presented his faith to the facts, and faith won! He is our example, and it is time for us to also "Faith the Facts!"

Don't Be Weak

In verse 19 we are told that Abraham did not weaken in his

faith. You see, a ninety-nine-year-old man may be a bit weaker in his body, yet age should not decrease faith but increase it. Abraham was always eager to obey God. I can just imagine how it went. One day God said, "Abraham, I want you to be circumcised as a sign you belong to Me." Abraham said, "What's circumcision?" And God whispered in his ear. I can see Abraham's eyes getting really big at this point.

I relate this in a humorous way, but we have a very serious issue here. We know that circumcision is no longer a requirement for God's people, but some people still practice it for various reasons. One time, a single mother who was coming to our church wanted her son to be circumcised but she didn't have the heart to be with him during the procedure. Even so, she wanted someone to be with her son while it was happening. She asked if I would do it. I said I would. I went into the hospital room with the baby, the doctor, and the nurses, and I stood near the little guy as they started. I was holding his hand, and they began. They tried to give him something for the pain, but pretty soon there was blood and the baby started screaming. At that point, (this has never happened to me before or since but for some reason) I started seeing spots in front of my eyes and my legs became weak. I had to lean against the wall before I passed out. Trust me when I say circumcision is a serious issue!

Again, as a ninety-nine-year-old adult, you would really want to make sure that you heard from God before you acted. Upon hearing something so drastic from God I think most of us would take many days to pray and fast. We would seek the counsel of leaders and elders in the church and read up on the subject. We would ask God for a sign—a really big sign! But not Abraham. Genesis 17:23–24 says, *"On that very day* (emphasis mine) Abraham took his son Ishmael and all those born in his household . . . and circumcised them, as God told him. Abraham was ninety-nine years old when he was circumcised."

Note the words, "On that very day!" That shows incredibly strong faith. A weak man would have stumbled and hesitated, but not Abraham. We may be inclined to put Abraham on a pedestal or think he is somehow superhuman in regard to his faith, and without a doubt we have to admire him. Then it dawns on me: We have a huge advantage over Abraham—*huge*! We have a book filled with the promises of God. He did not. We have the Holy Spirit of God living inside us. He did not. We have so much more that we can trust God for and have faith for in our lives. He had a simple promise from God that he would have a child. Someone has counted and said that in the Bible there are over three thousand promises. Abraham heard directly from God a few times over a span of many years, but we can hear from the Holy Spirit on a daily basis if we will spend time and listen to Him.

You might be tempted to say, "I don't have much faith." But this is not true. As already discussed, God has given every person a measure of faith. "Well," you might say, "what if your measure is bigger than my measure?" It doesn't matter because faith *as* a mustard seed is enough to move a mountain. You have faith! Now use it! If you don't use it you may lose it.

To make a muscle stronger, we must use it and then it will grow. To make our faith grow and be stronger we must use it as well. If we exercise our faith, it will grow; if we don't, it will atrophy. Abraham did not weaken in his faith. He presented his faith to the facts, and faith won. We cannot be weak either. We must Faith the Facts!

Don't Waver

The word used for waver here means, "to be in conflict with yourself, to hesitate or to doubt." In the book and movie trilogy *The Lord of the Rings* by J. R. R. Tolkien there is a character named Gollum, who seems to always be in conflict within himself. He is motivated by a dark force that compels him to do evil, but there is still within him a kind side that wants to do good. Throughout the entire story he wavers

31

between the two until his bitter end in the fires of Mount Doom.

To some extent we do this. We say we are Christ-followers and we respond to the message to repent and live fully for Him, but when we go about our lives, we find ourselves wallowing in old habits and sins. We find ourselves compromising in areas we know are not pleasing to God. We want the salvation that comes from the true God, but we also want to participate in the world's system of things. In so doing we find ourselves wavering.

Abraham was not this way. He stuck to one way of doing things—God's way. He did not lean on his own understanding or the wisdom of the world but leaned only on the arm of faith. Wuest translates verse 16 like this: ". . . he did not vacillate in the sphere of unbelief between two mutually exclusive expectations."

James uses the same original word for waver twice when he says, "But when you ask, you must believe and not doubt, because the one who doubts is like a wave of the sea, blown and tossed by the wind" (James 1:6). "Waver" in the original Greek is the word "doubt" here in James. Simply stated, Abraham did not doubt. He was not tossed to and fro in his mind. He was sure of God's promise.

In 1 Kings 18, Elijah was having a dispute with the prophets of Baal to see whose God was the real God. The people were trying to worship the true God along with Baal. Elijah went before them and asked, "How long will you waver between two opinions? If the Lord is God, follow him; but if Baal is God, follow him." It might be a good idea for us to ask ourselves right now, "Am I wavering? Do I doubt? Am I trying to live with a foot in both worlds? Do I want the hope of eternal salvation while giving myself to the ways of this world, which are not pleasing to God?"

Wavering was not on the menu for Abraham. He did not let the facts influence him, but presented his faith to his facts. He stayed focused on God's will rather than his own. So

Abraham was not weak; he did not waver; and the final thing we see here regarding Abraham's faith is that he was "fully persuaded."

Be Fully Persuaded

When we are fully persuaded of something, it shows. It shows in our actions and it shows in our speech. When my boys were toddlers I would do something with each of them that I have seen many other parents do as well. I would stand them up on something high like a kitchen counter and say, "Jump!" At first they might look a bit apprehensive, but with a little coaxing they would finally trust, lean forward, and jump. That tiny bit of fear in their eyes became delight as I caught them in my arms and hugged them close, exclaiming, "Woohoo!" The next time I stood them up on the counter, there was less apprehension, and soon they enjoyed it so much they would sometimes try to jump before I was ready. They would play this game with me until *I* was worn out.

Many of us have been disappointed by earthly fathers (or mothers) who should have been there for us. Sometimes those who *should have loved us and caught us* not only didn't but caused us additional harm in some way. The harm may have been through absence, abandonment, abuse, anger, criticism, shame, control, selfishness, and a host of other either purposeful or neglectful hurts that a father can inflict.

The mistake we are all inclined to make is that we juxtapose our relationship with God to our relationship with our earthly fathers. If our dad was absent, we may think that God is as well. If he was angry or mean, we may have a view of God that sees Him in that same way. Listen to me! Even if your dad was a fantastic dad, don't make the mistake of thinking God is like he is. Jesus makes it clear in Luke 11 that our best intention as a good father is "evil" in comparison to the goodness of God. Even the best parent will disappoint at some level—not because we mean to, but because we are human. I would never have purposefully let one of my boys fall to the floor and hurt himself, but there were times I was not there and they climbed up on something, lost their balance, fell, and got hurt. As a human, I couldn't possibly be there every time they fell.

On the contrary, we need to have a view of God our Father *as always there* and *always catching us.* He said he would *never* leave us and *never* forsake us. Here is where faith must find traction in our souls. We need to trust that God is good and cares deeply for us. We must become "fully persuaded" that He will do what he said He would do. This not only has application in areas of potential hurt but in the whole of our lives as well. God is pleased with faith. Faith makes Him happy. He wants us to take a leap from what we perceive as the safe place of facts and jump out into His arms over and over again because we are fully persuaded He will catch us. This is really what faith is all about.

Oftentimes the exercise of this faith is through what we say or pray. The leaping, so to speak, can be proclaiming something boldly that we do not yet see. "Claim something before it is done, and rejoice over it before it is done, and you are acting . . . [in] faith" (Roy Hicks Sr.). Isn't that what Jesus did when he fed the five thousand? He took the few loaves and fish, lifted them up to heaven, and thanked the Father in advance for what He was about to do. We absolutely need to do this more. We need to start proclaiming and thanking God in advance for the answers to our prayers. At the same time, we need to pair action with our words so that we will see results.

The story is told that back in the 1800s when the great missionary Hudson Taylor went to China, he made the voyage on a sailing vessel. As it neared the channel between the southern Malay Peninsula and the island of Sumatra, the missionary heard an urgent knock on his stateroom door. He opened it, and there stood the captain of the ship. "Mr. Taylor," he said, "we have no wind. We are drifting toward an island where the people are heathen, and I fear they are cannibals."

"What can I do?" asked Taylor.

"I understand that you believe in God. I want you to pray for wind."

"All right, Captain, I will, but you must set the sail."

"Why that's ridiculous! There's not even the slightest breeze. Besides, the sailors will think I'm crazy." But finally, because of Taylor's insistence, he agreed.

Forty-five minutes later he returned and found the missionary still on his knees. "You can stop praying now," said the captain. "We've got more wind than we know what to do with!"

How many times have we prayed but not added any action to our prayers. God is not reluctant to answer our prayers but he demands real faith, and real faith is always coupled with action of some sort. Remember, "Without faith it is impossible to please God."

I am not trying to be crude in any way here, but do we understand that ninety-nine-year-old Abraham and eighty-nine-year-old Sarah had to continue to be sexually active? You can have all the faith in the world that you are going to have the child of promise, but there was only one virgin birth and there will only ever be one. My point is that faith and action always go together. A person who is not weak and who does not waver in his faith is a person who is so fully persuaded that he continues to *do* something about it even if he does not see immediate results.

This is precisely what James says: "Faith by itself, if it is not accompanied by action, is dead" (James 2:17). True faith—real faith—will always have actions associated with it. If we say we have faith for something and don't do anything about it, it is not really faith. Even if the thing we are doing is to *speak* something out loud by faith. In Romans 4:17, just before the part about Abraham, we see that God "calls things that are not as though they were." We should too! When we come to the place where we know there is nothing at all we can do about a situation or problem, this is the place where we must have faith. If we don't, we won't see the promises of God come to pass in our lives.

Abraham's body was dead to the idea of having children, but his faith was not. What hopes, dreams, or promises seem to have died or, at the very least, gone into hibernation in our lives? Have we given up hope for the restoration of relationships? Have we lost our fight for financial blessings? Have we resigned ourselves that we are in a marriage that can never be fulfilling? Have we believed the lie that we will never have victory in some area of habitual sin? Have we given up the idea that we can have true and lasting friendships? Have we succumbed to the fear that certain loved ones will not come to faith? Have we lost hope for a child who has wandered from the faith? Is there an area of ongoing physical affliction that we have come to accept that we will just have to live with?

These are all just facts. Don't let them get in the way. Faith them! Trust in God for the things He has promised. Begin to call things that are not as though they were!

Stop reading right now and begin to proclaim out loud (yes, out loud!) what you are believing God for. Now, look for some way to put action to your words. Take a leap of faith. Father God will catch you.

It doesn't matter if the answer comes in
twenty-five seconds or in twenty-five years.
It has to come.
Facts are nothing. Faith is everything!
Facts are shadows. Faith is reality!
Facts are weak. Faith is powerful!
Faith is the evidence! So *Faith the Facts*!

Chapter Three
Faith and Direction, Part 1: The Spies

In a natural, practical sense, I am usually pretty good at finding my way around. Like most men, I don't stop to ask directions. I have heard it said that men do not like to stop and get directions because they do not want to admit someone might know more than they do. I'm not sure if that describes me or if I generally believe I have a sense about where I am and where I need to go (much to my wife's chagrin).

Some time ago, I watched an old *Home Improvement* show starring Tim Allen. He and his wife, Jill, got lost, and he refused to ask directions. Later he explained this to his "wise" neighbor, Wilson, over the back fence and wondered why men don't ask for directions. Wilson said that men orient themselves with directions, north, south, east, and west, whereas women orient themselves by landmarks. The reason that men do this apparently is that they have a larger deposit of iron in their noses that helps them to be more aware of their orientation to the poles. Later Tim tried to explain this to his wife . . .

Tim: "Some night, huh? You know, my direction is usually better than that. I just got all disorientated, even though my nose is all filled with iron boogers."

Jill: "What?"

Tim: "Don't worry, you got 'em too."

Sometimes my wife, Rhonda, and I will be driving somewhere and she will think we are lost, but I will always say, "Don't worry, I've got iron boogers!" To be honest, I have no idea if Wilson had any idea what he was talking about, but I like the concept.

The subject of direction is much bigger than we think at first, and driving directions are the least of our worries. Hardly anyone out there has not looked for some kind of direction in life almost daily. It depends on our phase of life, but we want to make the best choices in life, in vocation, in marriage, in education, in choosing a church, in friendships, in finances, in where to live, in what to buy, and how to prepare for retirement, etc. When we think a decision is a small one, we have the attitude, "I've got this, Lord." But if it is going to cost us a bunch of money or we think it is a major decision, we cry out, "Lord, where are You? I need to hear Your voice. I need to know what to do here." I believe we need to be led by the Spirit in every part of our lives so we can find God's best plan.

Get God's Plan

As we consider having faith for direction, I want to look at Joshua from the book that bears his name. His mentor, Moses, was the ostensibly the greatest leader among men besides Jesus Christ. Moses was amazing. He only had one little problem— a weak spot, if you will. He had anger issues. His anger as a young man caused him to murder an Egyptian and be banished from the land of Egypt. His anger as an old man caused him to strike the rock when he was commanded to speak to it and resulted in him not being allowed to enter the Promised Land.

Now, Joshua did not seem to struggle with anger, but as we read about his life we see that he also had an area of weakness: He was not careful in discerning or seeking the will of God. He says by his actions, "I've got this, God. You go back to running the universe. I'll handle things down here." Let me show you how this transpired in his life.

After taking over for Moses, Joshua did what Moses did forty years earlier and sent spies into the land. Moses sent twelve spies, and ten came back with a bad report, which made the people fear and caused the Israelites to have to wander in the desert for the forty years. Joshua learned from that mistake and sent only two spies. I imagine, before he sent them off, he took them out of earshot from the rest of the group and said, "Go ahead and check out the land, but, whatever you do, don't bring back a bad report." What Joshua actually said is, "Go, look over the land, especially Jericho" (Joshua 2:1).

Jericho was the city to the west, directly across the Jordan River from the where the Israelites were camped. Probably they could see the "City of Palm Trees" from where they were. You know the story: The spies crossed over and found that the people of the land—specifically the people of Jericho—were terrified because they knew what was coming.

> Then the two men started back. They went down out of the hills, forded the river and came to Joshua son of Nun and told him everything that had happened to them. They said to Joshua, "The LORD has surely given the whole land into our hands; all the people are melting in fear because of us." (Joshua 2:23–24)

I want you to note the response of the people in Jericho. They were "melting in fear." In the beginning of chapter 3, Joshua instructed the people to keep their eyes on the priests who carried the ark of the covenant. We might say they needed to keep their eyes on God because they were going to cross a river at flood stage. In verse 4 Joshua declared, "Then you will know which way to go, since you have never been this way before."

This is really what we are talking about here—knowing which way to go, knowing what to do, and getting direction from God. It starts with keeping our eyes on the Lord. We don't have to know what to do before we do it; we just have to keep our eyes on the Lord.

Joshua seems to be doing a pretty good job as the new guy in charge, but I would suggest he is operating a bit too much on his own strength, his own knowledge, and *trying* to be the strong leader. After all, he has been challenged by Moses once, God three times, and all the people again to "be strong and courageous!" This is why I say he may be operating in his own strength because, after they cross the river and are camped nearer Jericho, God confronts Joshua, as we see here.

> Now when Joshua was near Jericho, he looked up and saw a man standing in front of him with a drawn sword in his hand. Joshua went up to him and asked, "Are you for us or for our enemies?" "Neither," he replied, "but as commander of the army of the LORD I have now come." Then Joshua fell facedown to the ground in reverence, and asked him, "What message does my Lord have for his servant?" (Joshua 5:13–14)

Since Joshua had not consulted God about the plan for taking Jericho, God had to show up with a drawn sword. That got his attention! Finally, Joshua asked, "What message does my Lord have?" At this point, God delineated the plan for the attack on Jericho. After Joshua received the strategy from God, he led the people to do exactly what they were told, and everything went according to the perfect will of God. The walls of Jericho fell down and the city was taken.

Remember we are talking about getting direction in life. You and I want to know what to do and how to live victorious in this life, however, like Joshua, we stumble along, thinking we are doing a good job, when all along we really need to *hear from God what His plan is*.

You would think that after such a tremendous victory, Joshua would have realized how desperately he needed a word from the Lord before he set out again. The Jericho plan went off without a hitch, so getting the strategy from God for the next battle would seem like a really good idea. But, remember,

Joshua had a weak spot. I imagine we can all identify with Joshua in that we are thick-headed sometimes.

> Now Joshua sent men from Jericho to Ai,
> which is near Beth Aven to the east of Bethel,
> and told them, "Go up and spy out the region."
> So the men went up and spied out Ai. (Joshua
> 7:2–5)

Déjà-Vu All Over Again

Here we go with spies again. I believe the spies represent what *we do* to help us feel okay about our plans, instead of waiting on God for His plan then acting in faith on what He says. It is dumb to send out spies. What if the spies come back and say, "We shouldn't go," or "We shouldn't attack that city"? *What difference does it make what the spies tell us if God has said we should do it!*

At risk of repeating myself, I must go back to the story of Abraham and remind us that his greatest attribute was the *immediacy* of his faith. God said to leave, and *he left*. God told him to be circumcised, and he did it *that day*. God commanded him to sacrifice his son, and he left *early the next morning*. He never sent out any so-called stinkin' spies. But we send out spies. We think we hear from God to do something, and we go ask the pastor, "What do you think about what God told me to do?"

There are appropriate times to seek wise counsel, but most of the time we just need to have faith to do what we sense God is telling us to do. We think, I'd better pray and fast about this for a couple of weeks before I do the thing God told me to do. We keep sending out spies to check out the will of God, and, frankly, it is a waste of time. We are so afraid to jump into the deep lake of the will of God that we sit on the bank and merely dip our toes in the water. We say, "God, look! I am in the water." But God is saying, "Jump in!" Spies represent fear. Fear is the opposite of faith. No more spies.

Here is what happened when Joshua took advice from the spies.

> When they returned to Joshua, they said, "Not all the people will have to go up against Ai. Send two or three thousand men to take it and do not weary all the people, for only a few men are there." (Joshua 7:3)

Let me ask you a question. Whose plan did Joshua and the Israelites use to attack Ai? God's or men's? It is the plan of men, and here comes the result.

> So about three thousand men went up; but they were routed by the men of Ai, who killed about thirty-six of them. They chased the Israelites from the city gate as far as the stone quarries and struck them down on the slopes. At this the hearts of the people melted and became like water. (Joshua 7:4–5)

Now whose hearts are melting with fear? The proud and confident Israelites ran away with their tails between their legs. Thirty-six men died needlessly—foolishly. First Corinthians 1:25 says, "For the foolishness of God is wiser than man's wisdom, and the weakness of God is stronger than man's strength." This verse is not in any way saying God is foolish or weak. What it says is that, even on our best day, our wisdom and strength fall woefully short of coming close to God's. His plans may seem foolish to us at the outset, but it is actually the wisdom of God. Think about it. We look at the message of the cross as foolish. God comes to earth as a baby and later dies? What a preposterous story! Foolish to us, it has become the wisest and strongest story ever told.

Back to Joshua: The plan seemed simple enough. In the wisdom of men, two or three thousand of them should have been more than enough to attack the little town of Ai. But the wisdom and direction of men failed. Now watch Joshua's response: "Then Joshua tore his clothes and fell facedown to the ground before the ark of the Lord, remaining there till evening. The elders of Israel did the same, and sprinkled dust on their heads" (Joshua 7:6).

We can only wonder what would have happened if Joshua had consulted God about Ai first. Of course, after this time of repentance and prayer, God spoke to Joshua and explained the reason for the defeat. One of the Israelites, Achan, had taken some valuable objects from Jericho, which God had specifically said were not to be taken. This direct disobedience was sin, and it had to be dealt with before they went into battle. Once the sin was dealt with, they received the real plan from God.

> Then the LORD said to Joshua, "Do not be afraid; do not be discouraged. Take the whole army with you, and go up and attack Ai. For I have delivered into your hands the king of Ai, his people, his city and his land. You shall do to Ai and its king as you did to Jericho and its king, except that you may carry off their plunder and livestock for yourselves. Set an ambush behind the city." (Joshua 8:1–2)

Man's plan is: Don't consult God; just operate in your own wisdom and strength.
God's plan is: Listen to Me, and act in my wisdom and strength.

God's plan worked out perfectly. This time no Israelite lives were lost. The enemy was defeated, and the people of Israel were back on track. Lesson learned . . . or not. You would think that by now Joshua would now begin to understand how important it is to get direction and instructions from God before acting, but sadly it was not so. After the defeat of Ai, the other kings of the land began to conspire together in desperation to attack Israel as one. But one small group defected from the others and decided on another tactic.

> Now when all the kings west of the Jordan heard about these things — those in the hill country, in the western foothills, and along the entire coast of the Great Sea as far as Lebanon (the kings of the Hittites, Amorites, Canaanites, Perizzites, Hivites and Jebusites)— they came together to make war against Joshua and Israel. However, when the people of Gibeon heard what Joshua had done to Jericho and Ai, they resorted to a ruse: They went as a delegation whose donkeys were loaded with worn-out sacks and old wineskins, cracked and mended. The men put worn and patched sandals on their feet and wore old clothes. All the bread of their food supply was dry and moldy. Then they went to Joshua in the camp at Gilgal and said to him and the men of Israel, "We have come from a distant country; make a treaty with us." (Joshua 9:1–6)

It was all a complete fabrication. And what Joshua and what the Israelites should have done was stop and ask God what to do. But again, they thought, *Good job with Jericho and Ai, God, but we've got this one. We don't want to bother you with this.* So . . .

> *The men of Israel sampled their provisions but did not inquire of the* LORD (emphasis mine). Then Joshua made a treaty of peace with them to let them live, and the leaders of the assembly ratified it by oath. Three days after they made the treaty with the Gibeonites, the Israelites

HOW TO MAKE GOD HAPPY

> heard that they were neighbors, living near
> them. So the Israelites set out and on the third
> day came to their cities: Gibeon, Kephirah,
> Beeroth and Kiriath Jearim. But the Israelites
> did not attack them, because the leaders of the
> assembly had sworn an oath to them by the
> LORD, the God of Israel. (Joshua 9:14–18)

It may not seem like much of a mistake, but their failure to seek God's plan here resulted a difficult compromise and in the Gibeonites being a thorn in the side of Israel in later years.

Inquire of the Lord

Now, I have gone a very long way to get to one major point in this story: "They did not inquire of the LORD." Joshua lived his life always barging ahead, only consulting the Lord after he had found himself in trouble. I don't know about you, but I do not want to live my life that way—being bounced around by circumstances and bad decisions. I don't want to live by any contrivance of my own that is a shortcut to knowing the will of God, which His Word promises I can know. I think the problem is, we want to know everything all at once. We want God to give us a detailed plan of our lives. I remember thinking as a young adult how much I would have loved for God to show me whom I should marry or what school I should go to or where He wanted me to live. I would have loved to have been handed a detailed plan by God that described what kind of work I should do or what ministry He would have me do in my local church. Instead, what we find is a step-by-step process in which we must stay in continued relationship and communication with Him from one life event to the next.

In my own life, sometimes I did it right and inquired of the Lord. When I began to date Rhonda, I did some serious inquiry of the Lord, and, as I did, I felt it was His will for me to pursue a relationship and ultimately marriage with her. That was a decision that has resulted in a great marriage for over thirty-

45

two years and three incredible sons, who are serving together in the church with us. We have been in the ministry together for most of our marriage and have been graced by God to plant a church in the year 2000, which recently planted another church. We have seen hundreds of souls come to Christ through our ministry. We have seen God's blessings and favor over and over again on our marriage, and I believe it all started with *properly* inquiring of the Lord.

Sometimes I did not inquire of the Lord. Like the time I bought the 1964 Ford Thunderbird. It was a sweet-looking car, but let's just say it had a few mechanical issues. For instance, sometimes when I would let up on the accelerator, billowing clouds of bluish-white smoke would come out of the exhaust. It was a smoke screen that would have made James Bond jealous. That was actually one of the easier problems to fix. I can honestly say that I did not inquire of the Lord whether or not I should have bought that car. I am confident if I had sought His plan, He would have spared me the expense of all the repairs I had to make only to have to junk the car a year later.

Expect Direction One Step at a Time

I *do* believe we can know the will of God for our lives. At the same time, we should not expect that every little detail of the future will be spelled out for us. I asked the Lord about Rhonda and received peace from the Holy Spirit in that decision. At the same time, I did not know anything more than that. I didn't know where we would live, what we would do, how many children we would have, or if we would be pastors. With Joshua, the battles came one at a time and so did the need for more guidance from God. God did not give him the entire manual, *How to Take the Promised Land*. He gave him one chapter at a time, so to speak, and *only* when Joshua took the time to inquire.

Back in the winter of 1977, I lived at Camp Crestview with the caretaker family there. The camp is situated in an absolutely beautiful location near Crown Point, east of Portland, Oregon, high above the Columbia River and with incredible views of the city. I had purchased my first car, a 1962 Chevy Biscayne (another sweet ride, I must say).

One dark night after work, I was driving home and, about a mile away from the camp, I ran into the densest fog I have ever seen in my life. A wise person would have pulled over, left the car on the side of the road, and walked home. I was eighteen at the time, and wisdom seemed to elude me on occasion. I could not see anything in front of my car—no lines, no reflectors, nothing. I literally came to a complete stop in the middle of the road. Then I got an idea, I opened up the driver-side door and looked down. I could barely see the yellow stripes in the middle of the road, and so slowly, very slowly, I started crawling along. There was just enough reflected light from the headlights in the fog to see about three feet ahead and looking down to see the lines (please don't try this). Eventually, painstakingly, I made it to the camp.

Here is my point: Psalm 119:105 says that the Word of God is a lamp to our feet and a light for our path. We are going to get just enough light to see our feet and a little bit of the path, but it is a lamp not a one-million-candlepower LED torch illuminating the path ahead for miles. The fact is, we will only see just a little bit of the path. So God's Word will help us to know direction and know how to stay on the path, but, guess what, we must still walk by faith.

The New Living Translation translates Romans 12:2 this way, "Don't copy the behavior and customs of this world, but let God transform you into a new person by changing the way you think. Then you will learn to know God's will for you, which is good and pleasing and perfect." We will learn to know God's will! We don't have to get weird about this. We don't shut off the alarm clock and say, "Am I supposed to get out of bed this morning?" Get out of bed! But after we get out of bed and rub the sleep from our eyes, we need to have the attitude, "Okay, Lord, I am ready to listen to You all day today. I am tuning in to You, Holy Spirit, to hear any instructions You want to give me, and I will submit all my plans to You. I am not going to play games with You, God. I don't need spies to help me determine Your will because I am Your child and Your Holy Spirit lives in me. I am the sheep of Your pasture, and You said that Your sheep know Your voice. I am not expecting to know everything about my future, just enough to get me through each day."

Listen to the Lord

Late in the fall of 1971, I was thirteen years old and waiting at home for my mother, who was about eight months pregnant, to get home. Hours passed and I had not heard from her. Finally I got a call from my stepfather saying she had been in a terrible automobile accident and was in the hospital. She was driving her 1965 Volkswagen Beetle and had not seen a huge boat on a trailer that was stopped in front of her because the trailer lights were not working. She plowed into the back of it, and her leg was crushed by jagged metal. Also, the steering wheel collapsed and jabbed her in the stomach. She lost a lot of blood, went into premature labor, and lost the baby. In fact, she came extremely close to losing her own life. Two years after the accident, my mother left my stepfather and moved us to a little town called Winston, Oregon, to live with my aunt Mary. Within two months of the move, my mom, brother, and I all repented of our sins and came to faith in Christ.

About ten years later on a dark and rainy night, my mother was driving home from work on a highway at about fifty-five miles per hour. The visibility was terrible and, as far as she knew, she was alone on a two-lane road. Suddenly, she heard a voice say, "Pull over." It was the voice of the Holy Spirit. By now my mother had grown used to that voice and so she obeyed, even though at the time it didn't make sense. Only when she had come to a complete stop did she see there was a semi-truck with no lights on. It was sideways and blocked the whole road. Apparently the driver was trying to turn around and was still in the middle of the turn. She waited patiently for a moment then was able to go around the truck and come safely home. By being obedient to the prompting of the Holy Spirit, she very likely avoided another terrible accident that could have ended her life. It takes faith to hear a voice say "pull over" and do what you are told.

I can't help wonder how many of us have ignored the precious voice of the Holy Spirit, in one way or another, only to find ourselves in some kind of trouble. We seek direction from God, but, even if we get it, many times we lack the faith to act on the things we are told to do. Getting God's plan can make an enormous difference in our lives. *His plan* can keep us from being defeated, deceived, and disappointed. We can receive direction and we can know the will of God, but it will take faith to be patient and understand that we will most often only see a little bit of the plan at a time. We need to listen to the sometimes quiet voice of the Holy Spirit and, after hearing His voice, we must obey.

Let us learn from Joshua's poor example how to seek the plan and will of God for ourselves, our families, and our future. Rather than trusting in human wisdom we will trust in the wisdom of God.

In the next chapter, we will explore this theme further. We will see how foolish and potentially dangerous it is to let circumstances dictate direction.

Chapter Four
Faith and Direction, Part 2: The Doors

How Did We Get in This Mess?

Nine-year-old Danny burst out of Sunday school like a wild stallion. His eyes darted in every direction as he tried to locate either Mom or Dad. Finally, after a quick search, he grabbed his daddy by the leg and yelled, "Man, that story of Moses and all those people crossing the Red Sea was great!" His father looked down, smiled, and asked the boy to tell him about it. "Well, the Israelites got out of Egypt, but Pharaoh and his army chased after them. So the Jews ran as fast as they could until they got to the Red Sea. The Egyptian army was gettin' closer and closer. So Moses got on his walkie-talkie and told the Israeli air force to bomb the Egyptians. While that was happening, the Israeli navy built a pontoon bridge so the people could cross over. They made it!

By now old Dad was shocked. "Is *that* the way they taught you the story?"

"Well, no, "Danny admitted. "But if I told you the way they told it to us, you'd never believe it, Dad."

Well, we'd better believe it because the story is real. As we continue to look at Faith and Direction, I want to explore another perspective regarding getting our direction and plans from God: It is the idea of *open and closed doors*. In Exodus chapter 14 we have the story of Moses and the Israelites crossing of the Red Sea. (There are many scholars who think that it was some other body of water they crossed for various, sometimes very sound, reasons, but I don't care if it was the Red Sea or Lake Winnipesauke, the point is: They crossed through a body of water deep enough that walls of water stood on both sides of them, deep enough to drown all the Egyptian army who pursued them.) As they come to an impasse, God spoke to Moses and told him what to do.

> Then the LORD said to Moses, "Tell the Israelites to turn back and encamp near Pi Hahiroth, between Migdol and the sea. They are to encamp by the sea, directly opposite Baal Zephon. Pharaoh will think, 'The Israelites are wandering around the land in confusion, hemmed in by the desert.' And I will harden Pharaoh's heart, and he will pursue them. But I will gain glory for myself through Pharaoh and all his army, and the Egyptians will know that I am the LORD." So the Israelites did this. (Exodus 14:1–4)

The first thing I want you to notice here is *God's leading* brings His children to a place where there is no escape. They are hemmed in by the desert and stopped from advancing by a deep body of water, and God led them there. Not only is He leading, but He went back to the enemy and stirred up a hornet's nest. He hardened Pharaoh's heart so that he would go after the Israelites. They have the Sea in front, desert all around, and the chariots of Egypt bearing down on them.

We don't expect God to treat us this way. We think we should always be led to green pastures and still waters. We want to ignore the fact that *He prepares* "a table before me in the presence of my enemies" (Psalm 23:5). We think, *God, why would You do that? How could Your plan include leading me to a place with no escape? Why would You "prepare" a table for me in the presence of my enemies? Am I on the menu?*

I can begin to feel objections rising. *Oh, Pastor, that was Old Testament. We live under the New Covenant. Don't you know that God always leads us in triumph in Christ?* Let me simply answer by saying, how can we have triumph unless there was a battle? When we face difficult times in our lives we tend to think that God has abandoned us and the devil somehow got in charge. This is not the case. Our God never leaves us—never abandons us. Even when it doesn't look like He's with us, even when it looks like we've gone the wrong way, we cannot give up and throw in the towel. God is leading. He has a plan. He will take us through.

What we need to remember is, just like the Israelites, if we are following the direction of the Holy Spirit then He has led us to where we are. He has us right where He wants us because if He let us take the easy road to the Promised Land, we would never have the opportunity to see His power and glory manifested and we wouldn't have the strength of experience we need to do the greater things He is calling us to do. How did we get into this mess?—God led us here. Let's read more . . .

> As Pharaoh approached, the Israelites looked up, and there were the Egyptians, marching after them. They were terrified and cried out to the LORD. They said to Moses, "Was it because there were no graves in Egypt that you brought us to the desert to die? What have you done to us by bringing us out of Egypt? Didn't we say to you in Egypt, 'Leave us alone; let us serve the Egyptians'? It would have been better for us to serve the Egyptians than to die in the desert!" Moses answered the people, "Do not be afraid. Stand firm and you will see the deliverance the LORD will bring you today. The Egyptians you see today you will never see again. The LORD will fight for you; you need only to be still." (Exodus 14:10–14)

Moses appears confident and strong, but it is somewhat

humorous to me to see what happens in the very next verse. "Then the LORD said to Moses, 'Why are you crying out to me? Tell the Israelites to move on'" (Exodus 14:15). Apparently although Moses seemed strong to the people when he addressed them face to face, we must read between the lines because he must have started whining to God when he was alone with Him. The good news is, God can handle our whining. The truth is, whining really never does us any good. He has an answer to our problems, and I guarantee you it will be outside the box. It certainly was for the Israelites.

> Raise your staff and stretch out your hand over the sea to divide the water so that the Israelites can *go through* (emphasis mine) the sea on dry ground. (Exodus 14:16)

Go Through

God's answer to our problem is, *Go through!* I continue to hear people talk about living their lives by an open-door and closed-door theology. What this means is: If circumstances are good, God must be for it. Therefore I will go this direction. We say, "God opened a door." If circumstances are bad, God must be against it. Therefore, I will not go in that direction. We say, "God closed a door."

I'm sorry if what I am about to say offends anyone, but, seriously, this is spiritual laziness! We are not to determine God's will for our lives by what is easy or hard. We determine God's will by listening to the Holy Spirit. And if we listen to the Holy Spirit I guarantee there will be times we will face storms and trials—even closed doors—that the Lord wants us to fight through rather than turn and go back. Obeying the Lord *through* the circumstances is where faith really begins to shine.

What if the when the Israelites upon coming to the Red Sea lived by the open-door, closed-door modality? Obviously the door to the Promised Land is closed. God must want us to go back to Egypt. Oh really? No! What God wants us to do is listen to His instructions and obey Him. And if He tells us to go through a closed door then it is time to kick down the door and go through. We can't let closed doors keep us from God's promises nor can we allow open doors to seduce us into lazy faith. (Read the story of the prophet in 1 Kings 13 who did not obey God but was fooled into thinking an open door was the way to go.) Again I imagine a broad smile coming to the face of God as He opens the sea for His people and they go through by faith. "By faith the people passed through the Red Sea as on dry land; but when the Egyptians tried to do so, they were drowned" (Hebrews 11:29). They exercised faith to go *through* and this pleases God.

Know God's Will

God has a will for our lives. To ascertain His will, there are things He wants us to do and things He does not want us to do. There is a direction He wants us to go and one He does not want us to. Again, Romans 12:2 tells us simply, to discern the will of God we must *not do* one thing and we must *do* another. The thing we *are not to do* is "be conformed to this world." Do not be worldly. Do not be sinful. Do not rely on the spies (last chapter) to help us figure out what to do. Do not rely on circumstances to lead us. The thing we are supposed to *do* is "be transformed by the renewing of our minds." We pray, we repent, we seek God, and we renew our minds by reading, studying, and meditating on the Word of God.

This is what opens up our minds to hear from God's Holy Spirit and then we will know what His perfect will is. The Spirit may say, "Go through that open door." He may say, "Break down that closed door and go through." Sometimes, when our backs are against the wall, God wants to remove the wall. I would say, more times than not, we are supposed to go through the wall, go through the obstacle, go through the difficult things. Why? See what happened . . .

But the Israelites went through the sea on dry
ground, with a wall of water on their right and
on their left. That day the LORD saved Israel
from the hands of the Egyptians, and Israel
saw the Egyptians lying dead on the shore. And
when the Israelites saw the mighty hand of the
LORD displayed against the Egyptians, the
people feared the LORD and put their trust in
him and in Moses His servant.
(Exodus 14:29–31)

The result was they:
- Saw an incredible miracle.
- Saw the enemy completely defeated.
- Feared the Lord.
- Trusted in God.
- Trusted their leaders.

The benefits of letting God lead us from victory to victory
are many. The path of least resistance is rarely where God
sends us.

Deal with Circumstances

In the New Testament, Paul does speak of doors being opened
for him. In 1 Corinthians 16:9 he says, "A great door for
effective work has opened to me." God does open doors but
not without opposition or some effort on our part to go
through. Sometimes the opposition comes in the form of
circumstances. Though they may not be as extreme as what
Paul faced, we all face difficult circumstances from time to
time.

The word "circumstance" in English is about nine hundred
years old. It comes from two words. The prefix, *circum*, means
around, and *stance* means to stand. So, in a literal sense, the
word circumstance means "to stand around."

The owner of a large factory decided to make a surprise visit and check on his staff. Walking though the plant, he noticed a young man standing around, leaning lazily against a post. "Just how much are you being paid a week?" said the owner angrily.

"Three hundred bucks," replied the young man.

Taking out a fold of bills from his wallet, the owner counted out three hundred dollars, slapped the money into the boy's hands, and said "Here's a week's pay. Now get out and don't come back!" Turning to one of the supervisors, he said, "How long has that lazy bum been working here anyway?"

"He doesn't work here," said the supervisor. "He was just here to deliver a pizza!"

Our circumstances are just standing around, taking up space and keeping us from what God wants to do in and through us. Here are some circumstances we face in life: loss of income, health issues, loss of a loved one, divorce, relationship issues, etc. Our circumstances are the things in our lives that are *standing around* us (picture them as people linking arms to keep us stuck in the midst of them). If we focus on them, we end up just standing around with them. There is nowhere to go. They are standing around us, and we are stuck. However, there is one fantastic way to break free of the prison of circumstances, and that is worship. When we worship and praise God, we begin to get our focus off what is just standing around in our lives and on the Lord instead.

> Set your hearts on things above, where Christ is seated at the right hand of God. Set your minds on things above, not on earthly things. (Colossians 3:1–2)

> Rejoice in the Lord always. I will say it again: Rejoice! (Philippians 4:4)

"Rejoice!" The Greek tense of the word rejoice is really

saying, "Be rejoicing in the Lord; again I say, be rejoicing." It conveys the idea of something ongoing, already happening, continuing to happen, and happening forever. Don't miss the word joy in rejoicing. Be happy in the Lord—have joy! Paul is not saying, "Pretend you have joy." He is saying, "Rejoice *in* the Lord." Paul exemplifies this kind of life like no other person. Remember how he and Barnabas sang praises in jail at midnight. Despite all he went through, he kept on rejoicing and setting his heart on things above. In praising God and continually rejoicing in the Lord, we will find that our focus turns away from circumstances and we *break free* to rise up out of them. Circumstances by definition cannot move—they are just standing around. But we can move! And God wants us to move first toward Him and also in the direction He is leading.

If it is truly God opening or closing the door, we must properly discern this and act in faith despite what we see. If it is indeed God who opens the door, He will take us through to the other side where victory awaits. "See, I have placed before you an open door that no one can shut" (Revelation 3:8).

Don't Get Fleeced

I think Gideon showed us a poor example of how to find the will of God. He was told by God that he would lead His people into victory over the raiding Midianites. But Gideon was fearful so he asked God for a sign. The sign he requested was that a piece of wool fleece be wet with dew and the ground to be dry in the morning. God went along with this and did what Gideon asked, but Gideon is not quite convinced. So he asked for the reverse of this to happen the next morning: dry fleece and wet ground. God did this, and finally Gideon seemed satisfied that he had ascertained the will of God for His life.

When I first became a believer I heard older believers say, "I laid out a fleece for the Lord." (We Christians talk weird sometimes!) Over time, I began to understand that what they meant was they were asking God for a sign to get direction from Him in their lives. Back then, one lady in our church was reported to have said to God something like this: If I get a package in the mail today, then I will know that it is Your will for me to do such-and-such. The problem with her "fleece" is that it was not something miraculous. She apparently did get a package, but that could have happened any day.

This is a silly and, in my opinion, superstitious way to determine the will of God. To Spirit-filled believers I would say, "Fleece the fleece!" Part of the reason we have the Scriptures is so we learn from the mistakes others have made so that we might not replicate them. Gideon's fear-filled example is not the best way to get direction or confirmation from the Lord. If we use the "fleece method," we should ask for something that would truly be impossible unless God did it.

Finding direction from God by sending out spies, trusting in doors, and laying out fleeces is not how the Lord expects us to find direction. His method is listening to His Spirit. Hearing from God takes a daily walk of faith. What could be more pleasing to God than to have His children take the time to ask Him for His direction and plan for our lives?

Gate Crashing

As we finish this chapter on Faith and Direction, consider Jesus. Until we saw the results, we never would have dreamed that the Son of God would have to die on a cross. His very own disciples couldn't wrap their minds around the concept of a dying Savior until after the Resurrection. The devil himself never could have imagined that inciting people to put Jesus on the cross would result in his own utter defeat. If Jesus had taken the easy road, He never would have gone to the cross. But He went through the pain of it and the shame of it because He loved us. We who are believers tend to think in terms of the devil being after us. We talk about being under attack. But Jesus painted a very different picture.

"I will build my church, and the gates of Hades

will not overcome it. I will give you the keys of
the kingdom of heaven; whatever you bind on
earth will be bound in heaven, and whatever
you loose on earth will be loosed in heaven."
(Matthew 16:18–19)

Let me ask a question. Have you seen gates before? Have
you ever seen anyone attacked by a gate? Jesus has a picture of
His Church breaking down the gates—He sees believers
attacking the gates and going through them. Nothing can stop
the people of God and the true Church of the Lord Jesus
Christ. To further make the point that He wants us to go
through things like doors that are closed, He finishes by saying,
"I have given you the keys to the kingdom." What do keys do
if not open doors? I guarantee that you and I will go through
some difficult things in life. But know this: God has given you
the keys and the power you need to not only open but blow
through any obstacles or circumstances that are out there. This
is living by faith, and it makes Him happy.

Chapter Five
Faith and Finances

Money is a huge topic for all of us. I think there is hardly anyone who is not affected by the subject of money on a daily basis. Most of us try to be careful about expenditures. I read about one guy who wrote: "During my stay at an expensive hotel in New York City, I woke up in the middle of the night with an upset stomach. I called room service and ordered some soda crackers. When I looked at the charge slip, I was furious. I called room service and raged, 'I know I'm in a luxury hotel, but $21.50 for six crackers is ridiculous!' 'The crackers are complimentary,' the voice at the other end coolly explained. 'I believe you are complaining about your room number.'"

Somebody in Florida won the lottery recently. Five hundred ninety million dollars! As soon as we say, "They won $590 million!" the pessimistic people around us say, "You know they won't get it all. After taxes, they will only end up with a little over half of that." Awww, break my heart, only $300 million. I don't know how they will be able to get by on that paltry amount. Those pessimists also say winning that kind of money makes you miserable. Personally, I would like to see how miserable I could get. Seriously, I have never bought a lottery ticket and I doubt I ever will, but I can't help thinking about what good I could do with that bundle of cash.

The Bible has much to say about money. Jesus taught about it directly or indirectly more than just about any other subject. The reason for this is because of the connection of money to our hearts. He is very concerned about the condition of our hearts because He wants our hearts to belong to Him.

In Matthew 6:21 the Lord says, "For where your treasure is, there your heart will be also." The obvious implication is: The Lord wants to be our greatest treasure and He wants our hearts to be His. Unfortunately, in most cases, an honest evaluation will tell us that we tend to focus on earthly treasure too much.

In Matthew 25 we have the story of the talents. In this parable we learn many lessons about money but perhaps none more important than this one truth: If we are believers, *everything we have and are belongs to God* and we are only managers of what He gives us to manage. Keep that in mind as we read through this text.

> "For it will be like a man going on a journey, who called his servants and entrusted to them his property. To one he gave five talents, to another two, to another one, to each according to his ability. Then he went away. He who had received the five talents went at once and traded with them, and he made five talents more. So also he who had the two talents made two talents more. But he who had received the one talent went and dug in the ground and hid his master's money. Now after a long time the master of those servants came and settled accounts with them. And he who had received the five talents came forward, bringing five talents more, saying, 'Master, you delivered to me five talents; here I have made five talents more.' His master said to him, 'Well done, good and faithful servant. You have been faithful over a little; I will set you over much. Enter into the joy of your master.' And he also who had the two talents came forward, saying, 'Master, you delivered to me two talents; here I have made two talents more.' His master said to him, 'Well done, good and faithful servant.

You have been faithful over a little; I will set you over much. Enter into the joy of your master.'" (Matthew 25:14–23 ESV)

It is obvious the master in this story is thrilled with the faithfulness of these two servants who have done something useful with the money. The old meaning of faithful is "full of faith." In this parable, Jesus is talking about the "full of faith" servants. Often we focus on the one who was not faithful and hid the money. But this story is really more about the ones who did it right. Furthermore, the word "talent" sometimes trips us up. In fact, in the English language, we love to make more out of this story than we should, perhaps because the word talent to us means an ability or aptitude. In reality we need to take this at its face value. A talent was a unit of money made out of some kind of metal (gold, silver, etc.). There were different weights of talents in different time periods, but, in the first century, a talent could have weighed nearly one hundred pounds. We are not told what type of metal these talents were made of, but if we assume silver each talent would have been worth about $34,000 in today's economy. I believe it will help us to understand the parable better if we get the word talent out of our minds for a minute and recognize that the master in this story is entrusting his servants with *money*. Again, if we assume silver, the first guy was entrusted with $170,000, the next guy with $68,000, and the last one with $34,000.

Now, of course, we recognize that the Master in this story is God and His followers are the servants. As I have already stated, the first thing we must understand is that everything belongs to God. Our perspective as believers is that everything we have and everything we earn is all God's. This parable teaches us that God has given us everything and expects us to be wise and productive with the things we have been given. God wants to see a return on His investment.

Notice the one who had received the $170,000 went "at once." There is that faith concept again. Faith's response is immediate—it does not ponder, it does not wonder, it does not delay or hesitate—it gets right to work. The last one who had received the $34,000 was not a person of faith. He was not faithful.

> "He also who had received the one talent came forward, saying, 'Master, I knew you to be a hard man, reaping where you did not sow, and gathering where you scattered no seed, so I was afraid, and I went and hid your talent in the ground. Here you have what is yours.' But his master answered him, 'You wicked and slothful servant!'" (Matthew 25:24–26 ESV)

This is sobering. This servant sounds so noble in his excuse, but his true motives are exposed. He is wicked, and he is slothful or lazy. We need to let this sink in for a moment. Now remember, "Without faith it is impossible to please God." If we are not exercising faith, God is not happy about that. Even in our finances, if we lack faith we are not pleasing God.

Here is what God expects of us all. No matter how much we make—minimum wage or a million dollars a day—He expects us to be good managers or stewards. Stewardship is the responsible planning and management of resources. Remember, none of it belongs to us. We are simply the managers, and God's clear expectation is that we would manage *money* well. Let me quickly touch on four areas of good and godly stewardship.

Invest in God's Kingdom

God has set the standard of ten percent of our income as a baseline to give back to Him. In fact, the Bible refers to that first ten percent as something we *owe*, so we are technically not even beginning to give until we exceed that minimum. So, we *pay* the ten percent *and* we also *give* above that.

When we understand that everything belongs to God and He graciously allows us to use ninety percent, then we are thankful. Paying the ten percent is the wisest thing we can do with our money. God has attached promises to bless us when we tithe and to drive away the enemy from attacking our resources. Normally we are not to put God to the test, but in this area He says, "Test me!" If we are not giving ten percent of our income we are robbing ourselves, but, worse than that, God says we are robbing Him. That is something I don't want to play around with. It seems like we have more fear of the IRS than we do of God. Like in this . . .

When Pastor Harris picked up the phone, Special Agent Smith from the IRS was on the line. "Hello, Pastor Harris?"

"Yes, this is he."

"I'm calling to inquire about a member of your congregation, a Mr. Boes. Do you recognize the name?"

"Yes, he is a member of our congregation. How can I be of service?"

"Well, on last year's tax return, he claimed that he made a sizable tax-deductible contribution to your church? Is it true?"

"Well, I'll have to have my bookkeeper verify this information for you. How much did Mr. Boes say he contributed?"

"Twenty-five thousand dollars," answered Agent Smith. "Can you tell me if that's true?"

There was a long pause. "I'll tell you what," replied Pastor Harris, "call back tomorrow. I'm sure it will be."

I relate this as a humorous tale, but we recognize the truth behind it. For most of us, the idea of not paying our taxes is out of the question. Unfortunately for some, not paying God what is owed Him is done all the time. To be truly smart with our money we must start by returning to God our first fruits by paying the ten percent and trusting Him to meet our needs.

Some people ask if the ten percent can be divided up and given to various ministries, churches, or needs. I believe we should pay the "tithe" to God through the local church we attend. We are told in Malachi to bring the ten percent to the storehouse. The storehouse was a place for the storage of supplies, such as food. In Malachi 3:10 God says, "Bring the whole tithe (ten percent) into the storehouse, that there may be food in my house." In a primarily agricultural society the ten percent was most often literally food. It was the first ten percent of crops or flocks, etc. In our modern society the payment is normally money, but the concept of "food in my house" is still applicable.

The food can be seen in two ways. First, there is the spiritual food of the teaching of the Word of God. This is one of the primary functions of a church. We teach the Bible in various ways to people of all ages and so they are fed spiritually. Another function of the local church is to meet literal needs. This could be locally or internationally. Some of the church's resources are used to provide groceries to the poor or a corn grinder for women in Tanzania, as the ladies of our church supplied a couple of years ago. So the storehouse of today is the local church so there may be food in His house. The "full" ten percent is given to God through the church. This is not because God personally needs money. Job 41:11 says, "Everything under heaven belongs to me." Paying Him what He is owed, or giving to Him above and beyond, is not for His benefit but for ours.

Avoid Debt

We should not carry debt on anything except perhaps a house, and even that we should try to pay off as soon as we can. Avoiding debt means that we may not drive as nice a car as we would like or have the newest things. But if we do this right, eventually we will end up in a better place. For example: Instead of paying four hundred or more dollars a month for payments on a car for more than five years, drive a used car and put the four hundred a month in the bank to save for a car. In five years we will have $24,000 plus interest to buy a new car or, better yet, a great used car with low mileage. Doing it this way we will likely save about four thousand dollars in interest payments. This isn't just a good idea. The Bible says, "Owe nothing to anyone" (Romans 13:8 NASU) and "the borrower is a slave to the lender" (Proverbs 22:7).

Rhonda and I have never paid interest on a credit card. We use them all the time for convenience, but we have the money available to pay them off every month. Dave Ramsey, a well known radio talk-show host and author, teaches against the use of credit cards at all, and I think he is probably right about that. He recommends cash or debit-card purchases. This will drastically lower the risk of overspending.

One mistake I didn't realize my wife and I were making in doing things the way we did was to never explain to our children the fact that we always paid off the credit cards each month. All they ever saw Mom and Dad do was pay for things with credit cards. Some time ago I realized our error and even apologized to our sons for not explaining to them the whole picture. I have since made sure that they know that we pay them off each month and have stressed with our children the importance of staying debt free. I am pleased to see that they are off to a great start in life and are faithful with their money.

Get Smart

We need to take time to educate ourselves about how to manage our resources. We need to take time to read the Bible and look for the incredible advice given there. We need seek God's guidance as we look at ways to invest and save that provide good return for our money. Notice that the master in the story tells the lazy servant that at a minimum he should have put the money on deposit with the bankers so at least some interest could be collected. If the servant had done even this, he would have been accepted instead of rejected. So, again, being ignorant of basic financial principles is not okay with God.

Read some books or materials about good stewardship. Dave Ramsey's *Total Money Makeover* is an excellent place to start. Go further and get some financial advice from professionals. Think about saving for retirement when you are twenty instead of panicking about it when you are sixty. Don't rely on the government to take care of you in your old age. Rely on God and the wisdom He gives to plan accordingly. Finally and most importantly we need to . . .

Trust God

Even if we live wisely and debt-free, there is nothing that says the entire economy of the nation, or the world for that matter, could not collapse and leave everyone without a penny. We say, "I'll hide my money in a mattress." That is essentially what the wicked servant did. Here is the truth: Runaway inflation could make a million dollars in a mattress good for nothing but fire starter in short time.

In Germany back in 1918 the government went off the gold standard and started printing money like crazy to pay for war expenses. In 1924, only six years later, it took one trillion German marks to pay for what one German mark did in 1918. You could, in essence, take wheelbarrows full of money to the store and not even afford a loaf of bread.

We say, "That could never happen in the United States of America." Let's see, we went off the gold standard in 1971, and we in the last few years we have printed obscene amounts of money. Our nation is now nearly seventeen trillion dollars in debt, and the debt is rising rapidly. National debt has doubled since 2006. Every American, including every baby born in America today, already owes more than $53,000. And we want to trust in America or in the dollar for our future? No, my friends the answer is already printed on our money, and we must never forget it. "In God We Trust!"

The only answer is to trust God—to have faith in Him. Fear is the antithesis of faith. The wicked servant said, "I was afraid." It is not okay to be afraid. God is not okay with fear. We read in Revelation 21:8 a partial list of the sins of those who will not make it to heaven:

> But the cowardly, the unbelieving, the vile, the
> murderers, the sexually immoral, those who
> practice magic arts, the idolaters and all liars—
> their place will be in the fiery lake of burning
> sulfur. This is the second death.

You have murderers, sexually immoral people, idol
worshippers, people who practice magic arts. But notice what
is at the top of the list here. The cowardly! This is being fearful,
which is not pleasing to God. Now, let me put this in
perspective. This does not mean that if we blow it and are
sexually immoral or lie we will go to hell. We are talking about
someone who unrepentantly continues in that behavior.

We say, "I can't help it, I am afraid." God says, "Stop it!
Don't be afraid." If God gives us a command, He will most
certainly also give us the power to keep that command. God is
adamant that we do not fear because fear means we don't really
trust Him.

In a loving family relationship the children never wonder
if they will be fed if there is means to do so. My kids never
once were fearful that I would not feed them or take care of
them. In fact, if they came to me and said, "I'm afraid that you
will not feed me," I would be hurt and say, "Are you kidding?
When have I ever not taken care of you? When have I ever not
made sure you had what you needed? I would lay down my
own life for you and starve myself before I would let you go
without food." So, how much more is it an affront to a loving
and good God when we are fearful about His ability or desire
to take care of us! *No!* We must learn to trust God, and trusting
God will mean that He will ask us to do things with our money
to make sure we have learned the lesson that it does not belong
to us but to Him.

Robert Morris (pastor of Gateway Church in Dallas,
Texas) tells the story of God's blessings in his early ministry.
He and his wife were young traveling evangelists whose only

source of income was the love offerings they received from the churches where they preached. Once they went to a small church, which was the only church they were scheduled to be at in that month. An offering was received, and he was surprised to get what amounted to a full month's expenses.

Later that evening, God spoke to him that he was to give the entire offering away to a missionary who had also been at the meeting. He did what God asked him to do. Later that night they were at a pizza place. An older gentleman in a nice suit, who sat across from him, asked how much he got in that offering. Robert told him. The man said, show me the check. Robert was embarrassed, so he hid the truth from the man that he had given the check away. The man finally confronted him and said, "God already told me you didn't have the check anymore and He also told me to give you this." The man slid a folded check over to Robert that was for ten times the amount of the check he had given away—to the penny.[3]

We can't experience that kind of blessing unless we are willing to be that kind of giver. We either trust God or we don't. We say we trust God with our souls—to get us to heaven one day—but we don't trust Him with our money. Come on! What would we do if God told us to give a month's salary to someone or give it in the offering? Would we swat at the voice of God like some annoying fly buzzing around our head? "Get away!" Or would we respond in instant obedience to Him, knowing that He had better things in store for us? I suggest that if we have trouble with the idea, we have not learned the lesson that God is the owner and we are simply the managers.

If we are truly going to be a people of faith, then we have to be willing to trust God with our money and see His pleasure in it all. Come and share in the Master's joy and happiness because we have learned what it means to be faithful stewards. Let us deeply and truly examine our hearts. Where is our treasure? What do we trust in? If God told us today to empty our bank account for some good need or purpose, how would we respond? How quickly would we obey? Do we really see everything we have as belonging to God? Are we doing a good job of managing God's resources? Are we giving God the ten percent He is owed? Are we taking time to ask God about purchases or do we just do what we want? Let the words of the Bible examine our hearts. If something has revealed an area of sin, take time to repent right now.

Chapter Six
Faith for Healing

One day while I was in my office studying, I received a call from a man in our church. He said, "Pastor Sal, can you come to my house and pray for me? My back is in such terrible pain, I can barely move and I am unable to go to work." I told him I would be right there and drove to his house. It took him quite some time to answer the door, and when he did I noticed right away that he was hurting. He was hunched over and grunting as he shuffled back to his place on the couch, where he had been lying down. I sat and we chatted for a while. Then I got up, walked over to him, had him stand up, and, as I laid my hands upon him, I proclaimed his healing in the name of Jesus Christ. I stepped back and asked him to move around to see if he was still in pain.

He started very slowly, but soon his motion became fluid and he stretched backward and forward and from side to side. His eyes grew big as saucers and nonsensible syllables poured from his mouth. Finally he proclaimed loudly, "I am healed! It doesn't hurt any more!" He started jumping around and shouting praises to God. I began to thank God too, but I tried to hide my surprise because I have prayed for many people without results and this wasn't the norm. *It should be.*

Remove the Obstacle
Before we can talk about having faith for healing, we have to remove a potential obstacle.

There is an erroneous teaching that sometimes God brings

sickness or pain upon people on purpose to teach lessons or to discipline us. I hope to show the fallacy of that teaching because I believe if there is confusion about whether or not it is God's will for us to be healed, we will naturally doubt. And according to James, "[we] . . . must believe and not doubt, because the one who doubts is like a wave of the sea, blown and tossed by the wind. That person should not expect to receive anything from the Lord" (James 1:6–7).

Know Healing Is God's Will

When Jesus died on the cross He made a way for our sins to be forgiven. This is not automatic for everyone. To have our sins forgiven, we must first believe that Christ didn't stay dead. A dead Savior is of no use to anyone. Without a risen Savior our faith is useless and futile. Furthermore, to have our sins forgiven we must also choose to give Christ control of our lives. The word "Lord" is a title and means "he to whom a person or thing belongs, about which he has the power of deciding; master" (Thayer's Greek Lexicon) or, as I explain to younger children, Jesus has to be the "boss" of our lives. Now, if we will repent of (turn away from) our sins and accept these truths of a resurrected Christ and His ownership of our lives, we are saved from the sins we have committed. Our final destiny has been changed from hell to heaven. We have become a "believer" and "follower of Christ"—our sins have been forgiven.

Just because we have chosen to become a believer does not mean that we will never sin again. We may find that we have lost the desire for things we did in our former way of life and we might also feel that through the help of the Holy Spirit we are free from sinful thought patterns. Even so, we will still sin. If anyone tries to say they do not sin, they are at that moment lying, and lying is a sin! If we sin as a believer it does not mean that we have lost our salvation or are not truly saved, nor does it mean that Christ's death on the cross was not powerful enough to save us. It simply means that we live in a fallen world and though we try not to sin, sometimes we do. The Apostle Paul grappled with this dichotomy as well in Romans 7 and 8.

Of course, there is nothing more important than having your sins forgiven. However, Jesus accomplished other incredible things when He died on the cross. The prophet Isaiah foresaw the death of the coming Messiah several hundred years before it happened when he penned this well known passage:

> Surely he took up our pain and bore our suffering, yet we considered him punished by God, stricken by him, and afflicted. But he was pierced for our transgressions, he was crushed for our iniquities; the punishment that brought us peace was on him, and by his wounds we are healed. (Isaiah 53:4–5)

This prophecy in Isaiah was fulfilled with Jesus's crucifixion. Notice the first thing mentioned. He took up our infirmities. Infirmities are sicknesses. When Jesus was on the cross He was dying for all our sins, but He was also carrying all our sicknesses. The second thing mentioned is sorrows. Here we see Jesus bearing not only our sins and sicknesses but our emotional well-being too. Finally, Isaiah explains that He was pierced for our transgression and crushed for our iniquities. Transgressions and iniquities are different words for sins. But just in case we missed the point that the crucifixion of Christ covered *more* than our sins, he finished with "and by His wounds we are healed."

Later, Peter recalled Isaiah's words but he changed the tense of it, saying, "He himself bore our sins in his body on the cross, so that we might die to sins and live for righteousness; by his wounds you *have been* healed" (1 Peter 2:24, emphasis added). He changed the last phrase to say "have been" healed. I believe Peter altered the tense because by the time he wrote this some thirty-five years after the death, burial, and resurrection of Christ, the cross was behind him and the event that secured our freedom from sin, sickness, and sorrows had already happened.

Now, here is the point: Just as our sins are truly forgiven yet we still sin, in the same way our sicknesses and sorrows have been healed yet we still experience them. Why? Why do we still experience sickness after we pray? Why did my mother die of cancer at sixty-three years of age? Why do I continue to have pain in my back though I have prayed and had others pray? Why does a friend of mine continue to suffer with a mystery condition that has stripped him of strength in his upper body and limited his ability to live a normal life? When we hear of difficulties like these coming to adults we are troubled but we figure, *Oh, well, that is the way life is.* The questions get harder to answer when suffering involves infants and children.

One time I read a book that listed seventeen reasons why people are not healed. I was tempted to list some of those here because, frankly, there are some legitimate reasons why we are not healed. But when it is all said and done and we have done our best to remove any obstacles, we may still have unanswered questions. So why don't we always experience the healing that has been purchased for us? I don't really know. But I will tell you some things that I *do* know! I know:

- Sickness does not come from God.
- Illness is not His fault.
- He does not want anyone to be sick any more than He wants a person to die in his or her sins.
- Jesus paid the price for our sicknesses and sorrows.
- Jesus's blood is powerful, and healing comes through His name.
- Our healing was paid for through Christ's sacrifice.
- God's Word says that Jesus taught all His disciples to heal the sick.

- Jesus said that the things He did we would also do.
- I have personally experienced God's touch in my body in powerful ways.

As I previously stated, there is flawed teaching that at the very least insinuates God gives sickness or injury to us to teach us something or discipline us in some way. Oftentimes people will cite Job as their primary example or they will talk about Paul's thorn in the flesh. But each of these examples is clearly *not* from God. Read them carefully. It was Satan who inflicted the pain upon Job, and Paul's thorn is clearly identified as a "messenger *from* Satan." We know that God *can* and *does* work things out for good—so He can *use* sickness or injury to bring about a good result, but He is clearly not the *source* of them. Some would argue that if He allows something that is the same thing. I would argue against that. Let me explain.

When our boys were just learning to walk, we allowed them to have certain freedoms in our home. We locked up the cabinets where the cleaning supplies were and did our best to make the environment safe. However, we could not keep them from any injury whatsoever. With a toddler, there is probably not a day that goes by that they don't fall down or bump into something. And when that happens, we rush to pick them up and kiss their 'owie' and hold them. Sometimes when a toddler falls and gets a bad bump, the first thing a mom or dad will often say is, "You're okay." I often think, *If that baby could talk he would say, "No, Mom, I am not okay. It hurts!"* But I digress.

We all know that as children are learning to walk there are sometimes bumps and bruises. These help them understand things like balance and the hardness of certain objects (i.e., falling on carpet is different than falling on tile). And even though we know that the hurts are creating understanding, we are not the source of them nor do we in any way wish for the injuries. No *sane* parents want their child to experience pain or sickness. And yet there are those who paint God with a wide brushstroke that see Him as the author of injury and sickness or, at the very least, see the Heavenly Father as *purposefully* using such things to "teach" His children.

The clearest argument against this fallacious teaching, sometimes called "sanctification through sickness," is the fact that not once—never—in the New Testament do you ever see Jesus making a case for sickness. Not once—never—does He tell anyone who is sick or injured that he must remain as he is because God will get more glory out of it if he does. Not once—never—does Jesus cause sickness or injury of any kind and explain that He is using this to discipline someone or teach them something. In other words, if this idea of sanctification through sickness was something God wanted us to understand then Jesus would have, at least one time in His ministry, said to someone like Bartimaeus, "Listen Bart, you are just going to have to stay blind because you will have a better testimony to help people who are suffering like you." Never once—not even remotely—do we see this happen! Someone might object and point out that Jesus was unable to do many miracles in Nazareth. Let's take a moment to look at this.

> Jesus left there and went to His hometown, accompanied by His disciples. When the Sabbath came, He began to teach in the synagogue, and many who heard him were amazed. "Where did this man get these things?" they asked. "What's this wisdom that has been given him? What are these remarkable miracles He is performing? Isn't this the carpenter? Isn't this Mary's son and the brother of James, Joseph, Judas and Simon? Aren't His sisters here with us?" And they took offense at him. Jesus said to them, "A prophet is not without honor except in His own town, among His relatives and in His own home." He could not do any miracles there, except lay His hands

on a few sick people and heal them. He was
amazed at their lack of faith. (Mark 6:1–6)

I find it a bit humorous when Mark concludes with "he
could not do any miracles there except lay His hands on a few
sick people and heal them." How many of us would be
astounded and thrilled if we could lay our hands on a few sick
folks and heal them? To us, that sounds like revival! To Mark,
it was a low spot in Jesus's ministry. The lack of many miracles
aside, please look carefully at verse 6 and note the reason for
the few miracles was *their lack of faith*, not a lack of desire on
the Lord's part. Please take time to think deeply about this:
God is a good God! Jerry Cook calls Him a "predictably good
God." Explaining this, Jerry goes on to say, "A God who is
good in the way you understand good, not good in the way
someone redefines it."[4]

Jesus Christ, God's Son, did only what the Father wanted
Him to do and what the Father Himself was doing. John
10:37–39 expresses this truth clearly: "Do not believe me
unless I do the works of my Father. But if I do them, even
though you do not believe me, believe the works, that you may
know and understand that the Father is in me, and I in the
Father."

Here is a great question. Is sickness good or evil? Some
twisted theologians might try to redefine good and say it is
good because good can come out of it, but their argument is
flawed and I will tell you why. If sickness is good or if it is from
God or if God is in even in agreement with us being sick, why
do we take medicine to get rid of a headache? Why do we go
to the doctor to have him set a bone that has broken? If there
is a chance that this sickness or injury is from God, do we want
to be found circumventing something that God wants us to
experience? Wouldn't this be sin? Now we begin to see the
weakness of this kind of thinking. And so quickly the doubters
will run again to the story of Job to try to prove that God is
somehow behind sickness, but even the book of Job—Job

himself—testifies of God's goodness: "So listen to me, you men of understanding. Far be it from God to do evil, from the Almighty to do wrong" (Job 34:10).

I have taken a bit of time to cover this issue, but I hope that I have removed this obstacle that would cause us to doubt, and now we can get on to the *how* of healing.[5]

Have Faith to Obtain Healing

How can we acquire our healing? It is simple, really. We are healed the same way people in the Bible were healed: Faith! Let's look at this brief passage from Matthew 9.

> As Jesus went on from there, two blind men followed him, calling out, "Have mercy on us, Son of David!" When he had gone indoors, the blind men came to him, and he asked them, "Do you believe that I am able to do this?" "Yes, Lord," they replied. Then he touched their eyes and said, "*According to your faith* let it be done to you"; and their sight was restored. (Matthew 9:27–30, emphasis added)

The first thing that Jesus asks is, "Do you believe I am able to do this?" or *do you have faith that I am able?* Again, after we have removed the obstacle of whether or not it is God's will to heal, the next step is to ask ourselves if we believe that He is able. If the answer to that question is no or I don't know, then we need to get on our knees and get to know God better. In our hearts and minds, if He is not real, if He is not powerful, if He is not alive, if His Word is not true, if He is not loving and good, then we do not know Him well enough. Trust me when I say, *He is good and He is able!* Remove the doubt! Our God wants us well, and He is more than able to heal us.

Now, at this point, we may think all is lost. We might say, "I have known the Lord for ten, twenty, thirty, or more years and my faith is still the size of a small seed. I can't expect God to do anything for me because my faith is too small." Don't fret about this. Yes, we all need to grow our faith, but remember the story of the man who was paralyzed and was brought to Jesus on a mat? The men who brought him had to dig a hole in the roof of the house to get the man in because the crowd was so large. When they lowered this man, who was unable to do anything for himself, in front of Jesus, we read, "When Jesus saw their faith" (Mark 2:5). Whose faith? The men who had carried the paralytic. When Jesus saw the faith of the others He was able to heal the man. No one will be healed unless faith is involved. The faith may come from the person who needs the healing, the faith may come from the person who is doing the praying, the faith may come from the person who brings the sick to be healed, or the faith may come from a whole church of people praying and believing. One way or another, faith will be involved—somewhere, somehow, someone is putting their faith to work.

Let me finish this chapter by giving two practical examples of how faith can be exercised. Two interrelated stories from the Gospel of Mark give us further insight into how to exercise faith for healing. The stories involve two different women, one who was only twelve years old and another who had been sick for twelve years. Jesus walked into both of their lives, and His touch was life-giving and compassionate.

As we read through Mark, it is interesting how much detail the author gives to certain things while leaving other things completely out. For instance, Mark makes no mention of the birth of Christ but spends a great deal of time talking about Jesus's ministry in and around Capernaum on the northwest corner of the Sea of Galilee. It fascinates me when I see how much emphasis Jesus gives to individuals even when a crowd gathered around Him. I believe with all my heart that none of us is lost in the crowd to Him. This story and the one we will read in a few moments tell us something about how important we are to Jesus and how powerful He is at our greatest point of need.

The first way we can exercise our faith is to reach out.

Reach Out

From Mark's Gospel we read:

> When Jesus had again crossed over by boat to the other side of the lake, a large crowd gathered around him while he was by the lake. Then one of the synagogue leaders, named Jairus, came, and when he saw Jesus, he fell at his feet. He pleaded earnestly with him, "My little daughter is dying. Please come and put your hands on her so that she will be healed and live." So Jesus went with him. A large crowd followed and pressed around him. And a woman was there who had been subject to bleeding for twelve years. She had suffered a great deal under the care of many doctors and had spent all she had, yet instead of getting better she grew worse. When she heard about Jesus, she came up behind him in the crowd and touched his cloak, because she thought, "If I just touch his clothes, I will be healed." (Mark 5:21–28)

Allow me to stop and comment here. In the original language the words, "she thought" (here in the NIV and other translations) would probably be better translated "she said," or even better, "she kept on saying." We get the impression it is more like she kept saying either aloud or to herself, "If I just touch His clothes, I will be healed" over and over again. Sometimes we just need to be persistent in prayer. Not because God is reluctant but because we will not see breakthrough and answers unless we keep pressing in to the Lord. (See Luke 11:5–8 and 18:1–8 for examples of receiving what we ask through persistence.) We continue . . .

Immediately her bleeding stopped and she felt in her body that she was freed from her suffering. At once Jesus realized that power had gone out from him. He turned around in the crowd and asked, "Who touched my clothes?" "You see the people crowding against you," His disciples answered, "and yet you can ask, 'Who touched me?'" But Jesus kept looking around to see who had done it. Then the woman, knowing what had happened to her, came and fell at his feet and, trembling with fear, told him the whole truth. He said to her, "Daughter, your faith has healed you. Go in peace and be freed from your suffering." (Mark 5:29–34)

Let's face it, Jesus has something very important to do. He's on His way to heal a young girl. But, along the way, the crowd is pressing in to get closer—perhaps to hear what He is saying. The disciples, like robed Secret Service men, are trying to keep Jesus from being trampled. Just how this woman knew about Jesus and His power to heal, we are not told, but somehow she knew. Perhaps the stories of the healings that had taken place within the last couple of days had reached her, and so with great determination, she pressed through the crowd and touched the edge of His outer garment. The Bible says immediately her bleeding stopped . . . and then . . . Jesus stopped!

Now if I am Jairus, I am starting to get agitated. Time is of the essence here. We don't have time for these interruptions—but for Jesus, we find that people and their needs are not interruptions, they represent opportunities. Think about it. When the woman reached out and touched Jesus, she was healed immediately—instantly! Jesus could have kept on walking without stopping, and she, no doubt, would have still had her healing. He could have kept going!

One of the amazing things about this story is that when Jesus finally does find out who touched Him and He begins to speak to her, it seems as though there is no one else there in the crowd—just Jesus and this woman. What makes this encounter even more beautiful is to understand more deeply what is going on here. According to the Old Testament Law, this woman, because of her condition, was considered "unclean." She was supposed to keep her distance from others and not supposed to touch anyone. Furthermore, she has gone from having sufficient financial resources to having none. Mark tells us she spent all that she had on the doctors and still grew worse. Through no fault of her own, she was a social outcast and had been in that condition for twelve years.

Not only was she unclean but anyone whom she touched would be unclean as well. Thankfully, she didn't touch just *anyone* but *Someone*. And the instant she came in contact with even the very edge of the clothes of Jesus Christ she became clean again. It would be impossible for Jesus to become unclean by her touch because when she touched Him she was made clean.

This is all important to the subject of faith for healing because we are beginning to understand the heart and compassion of our Healer. Consider this: Jesus takes the time to stop and talk to her because He cares about her emotional and social condition as well as her physical one. He is restoring her to society and now, taking it a step further, He identifies Himself with her by speaking directly to her and using the term "daughter." In the original language saying, "Your faith has made you whole" is the same as saying, "Your faith has saved you." It means more than just you are saved from your suffering. He is restoring to her the dignity that God wants her to have. In so doing, He is almost certainly expressing that she has become a believer in Him and now has eternal life as well.

This is how Jesus feels about every one of us. We are precious to Him, and we are never an interruption. He cares about us physically, emotionally, and spiritually. When we reach out to touch Him, He will restore us. Like this woman, I believe that every one of us can reach out to Jesus at any time. What do we do in the times that we don't seem to have the strength to reach out? Those are the times we can . . .

Call Out
Now that this woman is healed and restored to society, Jesus can turn and get back to His original task of going to heal the twelve-year-old girl.

> While Jesus was still speaking, some people came from the house of Jairus, the synagogue leader. "Your daughter is dead," they said. "Why bother the teacher anymore?" Overhearing what they said, Jesus told him, "Don't be afraid; just believe." He did not let anyone follow him except Peter, James and John the brother of James. When they came to the home of the synagogue leader, Jesus saw a commotion, with people crying and wailing loudly. He went in and said to them, "Why all this commotion and wailing? The child is not dead but asleep." But they laughed at him. After he put them all out, he took the child's father and mother and the disciples who were with him, and went in where the child was. He took her by the hand and said to her, "Talitha koum!" (which means "Little girl, I say to you, get up!"). Immediately the girl stood up and began to walk around (she was twelve years old). At this they were completely astonished. He gave strict orders not to let anyone know about this, and told them to give her something to eat. (Mark 5:35–43)

Jairus is the ruler of the local synagogue. For the most part, as we read the New Testament, it seems the rulers of the synagogues dislike Jesus and want Him out of their way. I don't know if Jairus originally felt that way. If he did, I have no trouble believing that when desperation comes people often quickly change their opinion of God.

For example, I have often thought it interesting that the same people who claim to hate the police and call them names, etc., are the first to call when they get attacked or robbed. Case in point: Emmit Scott, sixty, of Roanoke Rapids, North Carolina, called the sheriff to say a man had assaulted him. Emmit said, "He had come to my garden and was stealing my marijuana plants," Halifax County Sheriff's Deputy J. M. Clark quoted Scott as saying. Emmit added, "I told him to stop, and if he didn't he was going to get in trouble." When that threat didn't faze the man, he called the sheriff. Deputies reported the resulting haul of pot from Emmit Scott's garden "the biggest marijuana bust we've had this year" (Roanoke Rapids *Daily Herald*).

Someone has coined the phrase "foxhole conversion." A foxhole is a trench the army digs to protect them during a ground assault. They can lie low in the trench and fire at an approaching enemy. The only problem is that when the enemy becomes aware of the foxhole, they may launch mortars or other weapons against the soldiers in the trench. It has been said that in a trench with heavy fire all around and casualties to the left and right, "There are no atheists in a foxhole."

People curse God all the time and use His name in vain. But when troubles come to their lives, they begin to call on Him. This may have been the case for Jairus. Troubles have a way of bringing us to God no matter who we are. Sometimes it is the troubles in our lives that cause us to reach out to God the most. Oh how I wish that it did not take trouble in my life for God to get my attention. Oh how I wish I would just call on His name with the same intensity in the good times as well as the hard ones.

Whatever the reason, this man has called for help, and they are on the way to his house. From a careful study of the text, it seems that this girl was not only his only daughter but probably his only child. Now there has been this delay, and moments later the devastating news of his daughter's death reaches him. Hope is lost. It is too late. Torrents of emotion no doubt overwhelm him. I imagine him turning toward Jesus, with tears filling his eyes—nearly obscuring his view. But as Jairus looks, Jesus gazes straight at him and reassuringly says, "Don't be afraid. Just believe." I can imagine that Jairus's mind races at that moment. He had just heard that his daughter was dead, and now Jesus tells him not to be afraid. Does he dare hope for the impossible? In a short while they arrive at the house, and the people are already crying and wailing loudly. The girl is dead, and everyone knows it.

Jesus takes Peter, James, and John into the house alone. The dead girl lies there, still and quiet. Now, instead of Jesus *being touched*, Jesus reaches out and *touches* her. Taking her hand, He simply says, "Little girl, get up." Mark loves the word "immediately." And what a wonderful word it is here. *Immediately* she gets up and walks around. Then Jesus tells them to give her something to eat. These two small details show us that not only is she alive but now completely well and whole— able to walk around and eat.

There are times we have the strength to reach out. Maybe we only barely have strength for it, but we reach out to Jesus to touch him and we are saved, healed, and delivered. Other times we may be too weak to even reach out to touch Him, but we can call out and say, "Jesus, come and touch me." And when the touch of Jesus comes, we are saved, healed, and delivered. God is still in the business of healing. He really "is the same yesterday and today and forever" (Hebrews 13:8). One missionary relates the following:

> Several years ago a missionary named Dean
> Truett was preaching and praying for the sick
> in an open air meeting in Tela, Honduras. A

man, who looked almost like a skeleton, kept arguing with the ushers in the service that he wanted to give his testimony. Finally, he was allowed to do so. After the service a taxi driver came up to Dean and asked about the man. Dean said he had picked up his chair and gone home. The driver was shocked and said, "That's not possible! That man has been totally paralyzed from his neck down for the last seven years!" Dean convinced the taxi driver to go to the man's home and see for himself. "He saw it with his own eyes and believed."[6]

The same power to heal a sick woman and raise to life a dead girl is available today. Jesus is still healing people in the twenty-first century. If you have a need, reach out to Jesus. If you know someone who has a need, call out to Him on their behalf. He is willing. He is able. God is good, and He is not the author of sickness. Let us make God happy by having faith and believing for healing in bodies, minds, emotions, and relationships for ourselves and others.

Chapter Seven
Faith-Full Families

- Did your life turn out like you thought it would?
- Do you have regrets? Disappointments?
- Do you have dreams that are unfulfilled?
- Have you become what you feel God designed for you to be in this life?
- Are you satisfied with your relationship with God, with others?

I was born in Los Angeles in 1958. My mother (who is now with the Lord) was having an affair with a married man who already had three children with his wife. Before I was born, my father and mother already had a son together who was put up for adoption. When I was nearly a year old, my mom moved to Boston—I think to follow my father. I think my mother believed he would leave his wife and marry her, but it never happened.

My earliest memory in life is from late December of 1961 when my baby brother was born. I was three-and-a-half years old. I can't tell you whom I stayed with while my mom went to the hospital, but I do remember who picked me up to go get her and my new brother: my dad. You might think that sounds normal to you, but you have to understand that my father did not ever live with us. In fact, I have very few (I can count them on one hand) memories of my father when I was a child.

Some time later, about the year I was in second grade, my mother brought another man home with her. He would stay the night sometimes. A year later he moved in with her and began to take some kind of authority role in my life. At first this seemed okay to me, but over time conflict arose in several areas. It was not uncommon for him and my mother to go to the bars on the weekends and leave me as young as seven or eight years old to "babysit" my little brother. I also remember waking up on several occasions hearing loud arguments and, on occasion, seeing fights that resulted in physical violence to my mom.

As if things weren't bad enough, they decided to get married. Getting married made a bad relationship worse, and now the "stepfather" was official. He was not good for our family. He was an alcoholic who would get very angry when he drank. It was the sixties, and they both got swept up in the hippie drug scene. Smoking pot and doing other drugs became a regular thing in our home for him and my mom. From time to time they would invite people over for parties. They taught me how to make mixed drinks, and I became their bartender at age eleven.

Things got even more twisted and weird. Eventually my stepfather admitted to my mother that he was bisexual. He brought pornography into the home and left it around where anyone could see it. The basic attitude of the home was "everything is okay." Any kind of sex was fine, any kind of drugs was fine, etc., just don't get caught.

One day in the spring of 1973, he went ballistic and threatened physical harm to my brother, who was eleven at the time. It got ugly, and my mom decided to separate from this man and move away. We had an invitation from my aunt Mary, who lived in Winston, Oregon, to come and live with her.

I had only met my aunt on a couple of occasions, but I really liked her. She was a believer and very dedicated. One time at a family reunion in Maine, I was playing darts with her. I was winning, but I got stuck and could not get the number fifteen. After several turns she had passed me, and I got really frustrated. Just as I was about to take my turn, I said, "I can't get it." She was a woman of incredible faith, and she spoke out and said to me, "You will get it this time." I wheeled around to look at her, and she stared at me with her piercing, blue eyes. I turned around, threw the dart, and got the fifteen. Her bold faith left a lasting impression on me that there really is a God.

Aunt Mary had been talking with my mom and told Mom if things ever got too difficult we could move in with her. So, in June 1973, my mom, my little brother and I packed up a few belongings into a tiny Opel Kadett and drove from Boston to Winston, Oregon. Upon our arrival, my aunt told us, "I only have one rule here. I just want you to come to church with me every Sunday." My first impression of the little church of about fifty that met in an old converted barn was: *These people are nuts!* It was your typical small Pentecostal congregation of that era—people speaking in tongues and prophesying, with a stack of tambourines on the front row for *anyone* who wanted to play one (hence my current loathing of the tambourine).

After about six weeks of attending, I guess we were starting to get used to the craziness, so when she invited us to go to some meetings at an Assembly of God Church in town we thought, *Why not?* We went to the meeting and came home that evening. We were all sitting around the room. I must not have been paying attention because, the next thing I knew, my mother and aunt were both crying and suddenly turned around to kneel at the couch. My mother began to pray and give her life to Christ. As soon as they got up, my little brother said he wanted to do the same. He knelt at the couch and confessed his sins as well. I was totally freaked out at this point. I thought, *What are they doing? They are getting sucked in!*

In that moment I had either a vision, or at the very least a thought, and the realization was this: *Hell is real, and I am going there.* It gave me the sense of scaling a cliff and almost losing my balance—a sudden and unexpected adrenaline rush. It scared me. I rushed forward and knelt at that same couch, repented of my sins, and asked Christ to come into my life. To be honest, I did it out of fear. (At this point I can visualize some overly pious Christian with a referee outfit on throwing down a yellow flag and yelling out, "Improper Salvation!" He's not really saved. He came by fear instead of love. That's an automatic ejection from Christianity! Come back when you get it right! Sorry, where was I?)

Before the moment of my conversion, I was a shy, introverted, and mixed up young man. Now, after receiving Christ, I was a *saved*, shy, introverted, and mixed up young man. But, over time, God has been gracious to me and gifted me with great friends, a great church family, and incredible leaders who have spoken into my life. He also blessed me with a beautiful and talented wife as well as three sons who have grown into incredible men of God, two beautiful and wonderful daughters-in-law, and, so far, two grandchildren, who are just awesome. My sons love the Lord and are very active in ministry in our church. All three of them play various instruments and lead worship extraordinarily well. Andrew, the oldest, is hard working and passionate for the things of God. Our middle son, Alex, is currently our youth pastor and leads in wisdom well beyond his years. The youngest, Abraham, is amazing. I have never seen a more trustworthy young man. My family makes me look good. But, as for me, I have found that God is a God who uses weakness for His own glory. God did this in me and for me by giving me a new life.

There is no way my boys would say I have been a perfect dad, but every one of them has told me I am a great father to them. I can see areas of weakness in myself, but I won't deny I have worked very hard at being the best dad I could be. Some might ask, "How can this be?" In light of your upbringing, there is no way you should have—could have—pulled that off. How could a person with no example or, worse, a bad example of fatherhood do a decent job of it? My answer is straightforward and simple. Faith! When I put my trust in God for salvation as a fifteen-year-old, I really was transformed and I started to study God's Word to look for examples of how to be a good husband and a good father. My conclusion and my goal was this: Be as much like Jesus Christ as you possibly can. Society expects me to be a product of my upbringing. Instead, I am a product of God's love and grace toward me.

How do we raise great families? In our dysfunctional world, how can we bring function and turn the tide of the disintegration of homes. The answer is faith!

In the Book of Hebrews, we have what is commonly called the "Faith Chapter." In this chapter we have a long list of names of people from the Old Testament whose faith stood out in one way or another. Baseball has its Hall of Fame in Cooperstown and football's Hall of Fame is in Canton, but the Bible Faith Hall of Fame is found in Hebrews 11. Let us start by looking again at the verse that is the foundation for this book.

> And without faith it is impossible to please God, because anyone who comes to him must believe that he exists and that he rewards those who earnestly seek him. (Hebrews 11:6)

Faith pleases God. It makes Him happy. When faith finds its way into family life so that kids receive love and acceptance growing up, God is pleased with that. When faith is displayed in dads and moms, children are given a chance to excel and grow into productive and happy humans. There are two men mentioned in our hall of fame whose faith deeply affected their families: Noah and Abraham.

> By faith Noah, when warned about things not yet seen, in holy fear built an ark to save his family. By his faith he condemned the world and became heir of the righteousness that is in keeping with faith. (Hebrews 11:7)

Have Faith That Saves
We should not romanticize the story of Noah too much. Let

us think deeply what it would be like if we had been told by God to build something called an ark because it was going to rain. By the way, to this point in history, it had never rained before. God created the earth with a built-in sprinkler system, and the Bible says that a mist used to rise from the earth and water the ground (Genesis 2:6).

So, as far as we understand, rain had never been seen, and if there were boats in Noah's time, there was most certainly nothing even close to the size of the one God described to him. Noah had immense faith not just to do what God told him to do but because he worked at it for so many years consistently. He did it because he had faith, but this text in Hebrews also lets us know that he did it to *save his family*.

What I want to ask us all, but especially moms and dads: "What are we willing to do to save our families?" Noah trusted the unseen God and consistently kept on working because he knew it would save his family. Today, many believing families have a hard time with consistent church attendance and keeping their kids engaged in spiritual things. To contrast, many of these same families would almost never miss a baseball practice, gymnastics class, or a host of other things that seem to draw families into an overly busy lifestyle. Now, in themselves, these opportunities for kids to participate in things that provide exercise, skills, teamwork, etc., are good. Don't hear me arguing against healthy diversions for children to be involved in. What I am concerned about is the lack of emphasis in some believing families to give attention to the spiritual life of their kids. With some, it seems that church and spiritual activities are often the first things to be dropped from a strained family schedule.

When I became a believer, there was a sort of unwritten rule that you don't miss church. Even when you went on vacation, you would find a church to go to on the trip. I am not trying to speak to some kind of legalism that insinuates missing church is a sin or displeases God. I would like us to ask ourselves what we are telling our kids about our faith and relationship with God when we only attend church one or two times a month. We show a lack of consistency.

Recently, someone emailed me and let me know they were going to be out of town the following Sunday. I thought, *Pinch me. I must have died and gone to heaven.* How extraordinary is that? Someone actually let me know—I love it! As a pastor, I was so happy to receive that kind of communication from someone. At the other extreme, I have people miss several weeks, and when they came back I said, "I have missed you." And they said, "I wondered if anyone would notice." Listen, not all of us pastors are that smart. Please don't put that kind of pressure on us. Let us know if you are going to be gone, and don't expect us to notice when you are gone. Sometimes we do and sometimes we don't. The point is that we, as families, learn to prioritize things that pertain to faith, like church attendance, prayer, the Word of God, and serving—and, like Noah, we stay consistent at it.

If every bit of free time is filled with things like recreation, sports, and entertainment we will find there is an emptiness to life. Think about it: Kids who have everything handed to them and are entertained constantly are more often than not spoiled and may lead destructive lives. But children who are challenged to give and focus on others are many times more likely to become well-adjusted adults. This is why committing to doing some kind of ministry together as a family is so important.

You know, pastors' kids sometimes have a well-deserved bad reputation for getting in all kinds of trouble and rebelling. And I wouldn't be honest if I didn't say I was concerned as we started raising ours as a ministry family. Now, again, our kids are not perfect by any means, but there has never been any major rebellion nor a time when any of them have walked away from their faith. As I already mentioned, all three of our sons are currently serving in some ministry capacity in our church. I think one of the key reasons for this is that we have prioritized serving God and have included the boys in our ministry. We did not see planting a church as something only

Mom and Dad did, but it was an effort of the entire DiMare family. What I am describing is not just for pastors but for everyone. Every person is a part of the body of Christ and each part is important to the function of it all. In the same way, families can serve together to fulfill some ministry so every need can be met.

The whole church is a family, and, just like every family, there are things that are not perfect. But church is a place people can find acceptance, love, forgiveness, belonging, and purpose. These are things that those around us are desperately looking for.

Noah worked incredibly hard for many years to save his family physically. And I would imagine that his three sons (three sons—I love that!) worked right along side him to build that ark. When the day of trouble came, they were lifted up out of the trouble. They were saved as a family because of the faith Noah displayed. How hard are we as parents working to save our children spiritually?

Have Faith That Obeys and Prays

The second hero of faith we will look at is Abraham (again). Here is what the Book of Hebrews says about him.

> By faith Abraham, when called to go to a place he would later receive as his inheritance, obeyed and went, even though he did not know where he was going. By faith he made his home in the promised land like a stranger in a foreign country; he lived in tents, as did Isaac and Jacob, who were heirs with him of the same promise. For he was looking forward to the city with foundations, whose architect and builder is God. By faith Abraham, even though he was past age—and Sarah herself was barren—was enabled to become a father because he considered him faithful who had made the

promise. And so from this one man, and he as good as dead, came descendants as numerous as the stars in the sky and as countless as the sand on the seashore. (Hebrews 11:8–12)

The lessons we learn from Abraham regarding family are many, but I want to highlight a couple regarding his faith. This verse in Hebrews tells us that God called Abraham to go to a new place and simply says that he obeyed and went. At face value that sounds good, but why is he so special? If we check a little deeper we find that Abraham's response to God was always immediate. God commanded him to pack up his family and go. Boom! He went. God said, "I want you to be circumcised as a sign of a covenant between us." Boom! He obeyed "that very day." God ordered, "Take your son and offer him up as a sacrifice" Boom! He left "early the next morning."

So, here is the first thing we learn from Abraham: Obeying God is more important than anything else. We might think Isaac would grow up rather dysfunctional. I mean, years later he could be in the psychiatrist's office, lying on the couch, saying, "And then there was the time my dad almost killed me!" Rather than grow up distorted, Isaac grew up to be a man of faith himself. The point is that parents who place God highest in their lives, above their own desires, spouses, kids, possessions, interests, etc., will produce kids who grow up to respect God as well.

This is the way Abraham and Sarah lived their lives. God spoke and they responded immediately and did what He said. Their own agenda was a distant second to the word they heard from God. When God called us to plant the church in Wenatchee, Washington, it was not an easy thing for us. As a young couple we had a ministry position as associate pastors that started in the fall of 1986. A year later we had purchased a small house in Ellensburg, and our first son was born in October. In fact, all three of our children were born in that town and brought as newborns into that house. Their little handprints were in the concrete we poured for a sidewalk. In 1993 we did a major remodel and added to the house, almost doubling the square footage. (Don't be too impressed. It started out at 962 square feet.) In 1999 we remodeled the kitchen, and Rhonda had her dream kitchen for the first time, but she would have it for less than a year as the call to start a new church came in December of that year.

I will never forget the day we finally moved out. The house was completely empty, the moving truck was packed, our kids were waiting outside, and we were standing in the doorway of the smallest bedroom of the house. This room served as the nursery for all three of our sons when we brought them home from the hospital. I do not generally cry very easily, but we both stood there with tears in our eyes because this was all we had ever known as parents and what was ahead was unknown.

As hard as it is to go into the unknown, we have been so blessed by God for our obedience. As hard as it was for our kids to leave the only home and friends they had ever known, they all agree that obeying God worked out far better for us as a family. When we obey God, no matter the cost, we are not ultimately led into troubles but into peace. We are not led to a dry and weary land but to the Promised Land. So listen to God. We must do what He says, and watch how He will lead us and our family into great places.

Another attribute Abraham displayed is that he cared deeply for family and interceded for them. One time his nephew Lot was captured, along with many other people, and Abraham went way out of his way to go fight against the enemies who had captured them. In doing this he saved his nephew and many others. It is this same spirit in Abraham that we find later on when God revealed that He planned to destroy Sodom and Gomorrah because of their wickedness. Abraham pled with God for the cities. He began by asking God if He would save them if there were fifty righteous people. And he worked his way down to asking if there were only ten would it be spared. God said yes. As it turns out, the Bible says there was only one righteous person in Sodom—Lot, Abraham's nephew.

From this we see that Abraham had the heart of an intercessor. Intercession is an interposing or pleading on behalf of another person or a prayer to God on behalf of another. Abraham physically interceded for the captives, and he spiritually interceded for Sodom. One of the greatest things we can do in faith-full families is pray for our kids. As dads, we need to hear this for sure. Any worthwhile dad would, without question, give his life for his wife or his children, but many men do not even pray for their families.

One time, when our children were still quite young, I came home from work and my wife was grinning from ear to ear. She said, "I bought you a birthday present." As I recall, my birthday was still some days away, but she couldn't wait. She handed me the gift which, though wrapped, was obviously a picture of some sort. As I began to open it, she said, "It's the one you wanted." Sure enough, I had been walking through our local Christian bookstore and had seen this picture on the wall and was moved to tears right there in the bookstore.

The painting, by Ron DiCianni, is of a father kneeling by his child's bed while the little one is sleeping. The boy is unaware of the dad's intercession, but the dad is unaware that just outside the window behind him an angel is repulsing a demon who would like to have access to the child. At the bottom of the print it simply says, "Spiritual Warfare." Below the title, James 5:16 is quoted, ". . . the effectual fervent prayer of a righteous man availeth much" (KJV). That picture was hung prominently in our home in the hallway that led to our boys' bedrooms. Nearly every night I was home, I would go in and lay my hand upon each of their heads, pray for them, and lead them to pray as well.

You can take everything I said about trying to be the best dad you could be for kids and throw it all right out the window if you don't have a dad's prayers leading the way. Even in the writing of this story I am again moved to tears to think about what hell would like to have done to my children but was resisted because of a father's simple prayers for his kids. To all the fathers and pre-fathers out there: If you are not praying for your kids every day, *man up, cupcake!* It is your job to intercede for those kids! Be a man about it!

Now, Dad's prayers are powerful, but I think there is something special about a mom's prayers too. We are so grateful to know that Rhonda's mom prays for us all the time. Mothers, trust me when I say your prayers are heard by God. I think God is extra motivated by a mother's prayer. Do you remember the wedding at Cana? Jesus's mother, Mary, said to Jesus, "They have no more wine." Jesus answered, "Woman, why do you involve me? . . . My hour has not yet come." I can imagine Mary looked at Him for a moment with a somewhat stern look that only a mother can have, saying with her eyes, "I am not taking no for an answer." Then she turned to the servants and said, "Do whatever he tells you" (John 2:3–5).

Prayer, in its simplest form, is asking. Jesus was, in essence, saying it is not time for Me to start My ministry. Yet, because His *mother asked*, He did it. If the prayer of a righteous dad is effective and powerful, I would suppose that the prayer of a righteous mom is at least equal but maybe carries a little extra oomph! Aunt Mary (who became a spiritual mother to me) never had any of her own children, but I know she prayed for me every day when I was a child that I would come to Christ and then every day after that for God's will to be done in and through my life. When I was still an infant, she came to visit my mother. She was a brand-new believer at that time. When no one was looking, she snuck me down the hallway into a closet, lifted me up to God, and dedicated me to Him. No one ever knew she did it until years later after we had all come to faith.

You don't have to have children physically to be a mom or dad in the Lord. And we all ought to be praying for the children of our church all the time. Some of them may not have parents who pray for them. If we feel the leading of the Lord, we ought to sneak into some closets with those babies and dedicate them to the Lord.

From Mr. and Mrs. Noah we learn that a faith-full family has moms and dads who are consistent and hardworking for the salvation of their kids, placing the children's spiritual growth higher than any other area. From Abraham and Sarah we learn that obeying God and teaching our children to do the same in life leads our children to have faith. We also see that intercession and prayer is caring for others. In a faith-full family we pray regularly for our own children and the children of the church.

Chapter Eight
Faith for Tomorrow

In June of 2013 we were so proud to have our oldest son, Andrew, graduate from Central Washington University with a degree in business. He was able to finish his degree while working a full-time job to provide for his family and continuing to volunteer at the church. He is an excellent husband and father. It is such a delight to see how well he has done and how hard he has worked. It seems like only yesterday he was the little baby I held in my arms and wondered what kind of life he would have. Life did not start out great for Andrew, as you will read later in this chapter, but by God's amazing grace things have turned out well. As parents, we all realize at some point that life seems to rush by us swiftly.

> Did you hear about the sloth who was out for a walk when he got mugged by four snails? After recovering his wits, he went to make a police report. "Can you describe the snails?" asked the officer.
> "I don't know," replied the sloth. "It all happened so fast."

As I sat at my son's graduation and took it all in, I could not believe how quickly we got there. It all happened so fast! For most people, one of the greatest concerns in life is our future. Depending on which phase of life we are in, our concerns may be about vocation, education, marriage, children, grandchildren, investing, retirement, and a host of other things we think about regarding what will come. It is certainly wise to give thought to these areas, but when we cross the line from thought to worrying about them, we go from faith to fear. This is where the Lord steps into our lives and speaks to us from His Word, and, if we dare believe it, we can live in peace with regard to our tomorrow.

Will you please read the following text out loud? Yes, the people around you might think you are strange, but there is incredible power in reading the Word aloud. Listen as you read to the words of Jesus here and let their truths sink deeply into your soul.

> "Therefore I tell you, do not worry about your life, what you will eat or drink; or about your body, what you will wear. Is not life more than food, and the body more than clothes? Look at the birds of the air; they do not sow or reap or store away in barns, and yet your heavenly Father feeds them. Are you not much more valuable than they? Can any one of you by worrying add a single hour to your life? And why do you worry about clothes? See how the flowers of the field grow. They do not labor or spin. Yet I tell you that not even Solomon in all his splendor was dressed like one of these. If that is how God clothes the grass of the field, which is here today and tomorrow is thrown into the fire, will He not much more clothe you—you of little faith? So do not worry, saying, 'What shall we eat?' or 'What shall we drink?' or 'What shall we wear?' For the pagans run after all these things, and your heavenly Father knows that you need them. But seek first his kingdom and his righteousness, and all these things will be given to you as well. Therefore do not worry about tomorrow, for

tomorrow will worry about itself. Each day has enough trouble of its own." (Matthew 6:25–34)

In this passage Jesus addresses our propensity to worry and be fearful about everything from the most basic of necessities to life itself, which can be summed up in the word *tomorrow*. When we worry, we don't generally worry about the past or even today because we have made it this far and what is done is done. But we wonder about tomorrow.

Face Tomorrow's Problems

In 1999 we had the big Y2K scare. Many people were convinced the world was going to go into complete chaos because the original computer programmers didn't think far enough ahead and only used two digits to represent the year. Some feared that when the computers switched over to the year 2000 the digits 00 would freak the computers, starting a cascade of failures and glitches that would cause problems everywhere, including the possibility of shutting down power plants and maybe even launching nuclear missiles.

Frightened people stocked up on food supplies, bottled water, and extra guns, according to news reports. One well-known preacher "prophesied the electronic equivalent of fire and brimstone: 'I believe that Y2K may be God's instrument to shake this nation, humble this nation, awaken this nation and from this nation start revival that spreads the face of the earth before the Rapture of the Church.'"[7] (By the way, I am certainly not opposed to us being prepared, even stocking up on food or other necessities. There is a level of wisdom in being ready for storms, outages, or other unforeseen problems. Some of us may feel led by God to be ready for extended shortages. However, if our motivation is fear-based or worry-based, it is sin.)

With these kinds of warnings in the news, there were people in churches all around who were stocking up on food supplies and filling gallon jugs of water and storing them around the house. I remember watching all this and thinking about what Jesus said in Matthew 6, "Don't worry about what you will eat . . . or drink . . . or wear." His whole conclusion of the matter is found in verse 34, "Therefore do not worry about tomorrow, for tomorrow will worry about itself. Each day has enough trouble of its own." Let tomorrow worry about itself since it does us no good to be fearful when, because of God's promises, we can be faith-filled about the next day.

Notice at the end of verse 30, Jesus chastises people who are worrying, saying it is because they have *little faith*. Remember, when we are new believers it is acceptable to have little faith, to have faith the size of a mustard seed. But Christ's expectation of us is that we have faith that grows. Little faith won't cut it for a so-called mature believer. We need mustard-*tree* faith so that we don't allow worry to paralyze our tomorrows.

On October 15, 1987, our first son, Andrew, was born. Rhonda had labored for many hours and was incredibly brave, but as time went on well past anything that could be expected, the doctor finally announced that she would have to have a Caesarean section. This was not how things were supposed to go. We are people of faith and were convinced that everything would go along normally. But it was not to be. Soon we were in the operating room and the doctors began the surgery. After they had prepped her, I was escorted in to be seated at a place by her head. One of the first things they did was to set up a sort of tent between our heads and her abdomen. It was obvious the tent was there for our benefit so we did not see what was going on, which was just as well as far as I was concerned.

It didn't take very long for them to make the incision and begin to work at delivering the baby. All the while the anesthesiologist kept track of Rhonda's pain and any level of discomfort or nausea. I did the best job I could just holding her hand and trying to speak reassuringly to her. I had it in my mind that soon we would see our baby. This was before the time of ultrasounds being a normal part of prenatal care, and we had no idea if we were having a boy or a girl. Before very long (after a lot of grotesque squishing sounds), they announced it was a boy. At that moment, I expected them to show us the baby, but they did not.

It was not at all like what you see in the movies, where they hand the messy child to the mom, but I figured they must do things differently with a c-section. So, we waited a couple of minutes as they started to close the incision. Soon Dr. Vernie, the pediatrician who was assisting, came in the room and asked me to come with him. Just as we got into the hallway, out of earshot of Rhonda, the first words out of his mouth were, "We have a problem."

That moment, frozen in my memory, was intense. I felt that all my blood drained out of my body somewhere and my head spun. None of this was going as expected. My mind raced to think of what he could mean as he led me to my son, who had a couple of nurses working on him. The doctor went on to explain that part of Andrew's intestines was looped out of his body and into his umbilical cord. They left the cut umbilical cord longer than usual and were in the process of wrapping a gauze bandage around his abdomen. Dr. Vernie went on to explain that sometimes this kind of birth defect . . . (Did he just say "birth defect"? What little strength I thought I had left was now slipping away.) He said, "Sometimes this kind of birth defect indicates further abnormalities and possibly other organs may be affected." He continued, "He is going to need immediate surgery, and our facilities are not equipped for this. We are calling to arrange for him to be airlifted to Children's Hospital in Seattle."

By this time they had Andrew all bandaged up and were talking about taking him back into the surgery area so that Rhonda could see him for the first time. They handed him to me, and I held my boy in my arms for the first time. He seemed peaceful and perfect to me. All his fingers and toes were accounted for. We walked together into the room where they were finishing up with Rhonda, and I brought him over for her to see. Between Dr. Vernie and me, we explained the problem to her. Tears welled up in her eyes as she realized that her newborn son was going to be taken from her in just a few moments. This was not how it was supposed to go!

She kissed him goodbye, and they took him to get him ready for the trip. The doctors began to talk to me about what I was going to do. Did I want to stay with Rhonda or go with the baby to Seattle? What a gut-wrenching decision that was. I love my wife and I felt so sorry for her, but her mother was there with her. For the first time in my life, I felt what it meant to be a dad. I was concerned that my infant son would be going through this ordeal with no one who loved him beside him. As difficult a decision as it was, I decided to go with Andrew. I think Rhonda was actually reassured by that decision as well.

Within a few hours, Andrew went into surgery and I collapsed from exhaustion in the waiting room. I felt like I had only been asleep for fifteen minutes when a kind-faced doctor with cartoon characters on his surgeon's cap woke me up. It had been four hours. He told me the surgery was a success. They were able to make a small incision around where his belly button would be and ease the loop of intestines back into his body. While they were doing this, they took a look around with a scope and verified that his other organs were completely normal. (Although he did tell my they couldn't find Andrew's appendix in its normal location. They weren't sure if it wasn't there at all or just in a different spot. Good thing we don't necessarily need that one.)

Rhonda, clutching at her midsection with a pillow, courageously joined him two days later. Andrew was in the hospital for about a week, and, when he was cleared by the doctors, we took him home.

When we face the unexpected in our lives, it can be deeply troubling. If everything goes positively, as we expect, we are at peace. The word "expect" speaks of the future, it speaks of tomorrow. If we are reasonably sure that things will go along normally, we don't tend to have worries. But if something happens that causes us to question our hopes, we can begin to flail and experience apprehension.

Our experience with Andrew pales in comparison to some of the terrible difficulties I have seen others go through. A few years ago a couple in our church endured their firstborn son, Lincoln, being born with severe Down Syndrome and a hole in his heart. They could do little but care for and comfort their precious son as they watched his life ebb away slowly over a period of three months. This kind of tragedy is overwhelmingly sad and challenging. Words fail. Many times the only thing we can do in those situations is weep with those who weep. In those dark times, our hope can ebb and our vision for tomorrow can be obscured.

In times of difficulty we cannot succumb to complete despair. Problems will come to everyone in various ways and intensity. This is the time for faith. Faith is all about the future. Faith is all about the unseen. Faith is all about potential!

Embrace Tomorrow's Potential
The apostle James presses us to go even further in our faith by understanding that nothing is for sure and life is short.

> Now listen, you who say, "Today or tomorrow we will go to this or that city, spend a year there, carry on business and make money." Why, you do not even know what will happen tomorrow. What is your life? You are a mist that appears for a little while and then vanishes. Instead, you ought to say, "If it is the Lord's will, we will live and do this or that." (James 4:13–16)

Understanding the brevity of this life actually gives us the strength we need to experience tomorrow's potential. Once we have the mindset that life is brief, even the most difficult of trials we face seem to lose much of their pain. I am not minimizing the loss of a child or the betrayal of a business partner. I am not saying that divorce does not hurt or that a physical problem does not deeply affect our lives. But if we can get a perspective that says, "Life is a mist, here for a little while and then vanishes," we will begin to put our focus on what is real and what is eternal.

Thomas Edison invented the microphone, the phonograph, the incandescent light, the storage battery, talking movies, and more than one thousand other things. As of 1914 he had worked for ten years on a storage battery. This greatly strained his finances. One particular evening, spontaneous combustion had broken out in the film room. Within minutes all the packing compounds, celluloid for records and film, and other flammable goods were in flames. Fire companies from eight surrounding towns arrived, but the heat was so intense and the water pressure so low that the attempt to douse the flames was futile. Everything was destroyed. With all his assets going up in a whoosh (although the damage exceeded two million dollars, the buildings were only insured for $238,000 because they were made of concrete and thought to be fireproof), would his spirit be broken?

The inventor's twenty-four-year-old son, Charles, searched frantically for his father. He finally found him, calmly watching the fire, his face glowing in the reflection, his white hair blowing in the wind. "My heart ached for him," said Charles. "He was sixty-seven —no longer a young man—and everything was going up in flames." The next morning, Thomas Edison looked at the ruins and said, "There is great value in disaster. All our mistakes are burned up. Thank God, we can start anew." Three weeks after the fire, he managed to deliver the first phonograph.[8]

Tomorrow's potential is found in our trusting God with reckless abandon. What if everything we had vanished today? Would we become depressed or despondent? Would we just give up and walk away? If our answer to these questions is "Yes," I would suggest we do not have the kind of faith in God that we need. This life seems permanent and so real to us, but remember James says it is a vapor.

Warren Wiersbe said, "Boasting about an unknown future is sin. Yet so many people make their plans without praying or seeking the mind of God. They live like the worldly sinner who thinks he has security for the future, but discovers he has lost everything." [9]

We will only find potential for tomorrow as we have faith in God. Some might mistakenly think that I am saying "Don't plan for the future," but this is not what I am saying. Jesus said that the birds don't sow or reap or store away in barns, but we do and we should. What Jesus means is, don't put your trust in the things that you sow or reap or put in barns because at the end of the day *it is God who feeds you and sustains you.* If it all vanished tomorrow, we should not despair but be hopeful to see how our Heavenly Father is going to take care of us. The potential is great if we get our focus right. The Bible says that the mercies of the Lord are new every morning. No matter what happened yesterday, today's potential is fresh. Like Thomas Edison, we can say everyday, "Thank God we can start anew!"

What will get us through the difficulties we face? Faith! Faith for tomorrow! Faith to trust God for a brighter, richer, and more fulfilling future than we have experienced to date. What is the object of such faith? It is Christ and Christ alone.

Please don't make the mistake of putting faith in faith. The object of our faith is Jesus Christ. Again, Jesus said, "anyone who has faith *in Me*" (emphasis mine).

When it was time to pick up Andrew and Rhonda at the hospital to bring them home, I made the two-hour drive across the mountain pass to Seattle. As I drove along, an old song began to rise up in my heart. Straining to see the road ahead through my tears, I sang it at the top of my lungs . . .

> Pardon for sin and a peace that endureth,
> Thy own dear presence to cheer and to guide;
> Strength for today and bright hope for tomorrow,

(When I hit that line of the song, I bawled like a baby. I don't know if anyone saw me in my car singing and crying. To tell you the truth, I couldn't care less. At that moment I knew God was with me and I had faith for tomorrow.)

> Blessings all mine, with ten thousand beside!
> Great is Thy faithfulness!
> Great is Thy faithfulness!
> Morning by morning new mercies I see;
> All I have needed Thy hand hath provided;
> Great is Thy faithfulness, Lord unto me.[10]

Somehow I knew that Andrew was going to be okay. I could wish that he had never been born with that defect, and I could wish that by faith I laid hands on him and watched an instantaneous miracle happen before my eyes. And I will not stop contending for these miracles in my life, but when I don't see them it is comforting to know that God has my tomorrow in His hands. This is what gives us "strength for today and bright hope for tomorrow." So, do as the Lord says, "Don't worry about tomorrow." This is only possible as we put our tomorrow in the Lord's hands and trust Him with our future. Let tomorrow worry about tomorrow, and we will trust in the

Lord.

As we talk about faith for tomorrow, we must recognize that one day, I believe very soon, we will hear a loud trumpet blast. Before we even have a chance to think about it, we will all be changed and will go up to meet the Lord Jesus in the air to be with Him forever. The Lord is coming soon, and He has promised to take us to our *real* home, to our *real* future. As we continue to have faith for tomorrow, let us never lose sight of the ultimate tomorrow and the soon coming of our Lord for those who have put their faith in Him for salvation.

Finally, let me say, there is only *one thing* anyone should worry about. Those who have not made Christ the Lord of their lives, or have wandered away from the faith, or don't know whether they are truly saved should worry about tomorrow. The promise of a secure and glorious tomorrow is only made to believers, who have been forgiven of their sins. Jesus told a story about a man who thought he had it all. This man even said to himself, "'You have plenty of grain laid up for many years. Take life easy; eat, drink and be merry.' But God said to him, 'You fool! This very night your life will be demanded from you. Then who will get what you have prepared for yourself?' This is how it will be with whoever stores up things for themselves but is not rich toward God" (Luke 12:19–21).

What if your life ended today? Are you ready to step into eternity? If you are not certain, please turn to the last chapter of this book, titled "Saving Faith," and read it now. Get your heart and life right with God so that you too can have faith for tomorrow.

Chapter Nine
Faith to Rest

The principle of rest is so important to God that in the work of Creation *and* in the work of Salvation, God Himself rested. The Hebrew word for rest is *shabat* from which we get the word Sabbath. Sabbath is both a day and a principle. We see many references in the Gospels to things happening on the Sabbath. For example:

> One Sabbath Jesus was going through the grainfields, and as his disciples walked along, they began to pick some heads of grain. The Pharisees said to him, "Look, why are they doing what is unlawful on the Sabbath?" He answered, "Have you never read what David did when he and his companions were hungry and in need? In the days of Abiathar the high priest, he entered the house of God and ate the consecrated bread, which is lawful only for priests to eat. And he also gave some to his companions." Then he said to them, "The Sabbath was made for man, not man for the Sabbath. So the Son of Man is Lord even of the Sabbath." (Mark 2:23–28)

Here Jesus is making sure we recognize God's good intentions for humankind when He made the Sabbath. We don't want to miss this gift from God to us by relegating it to something from the Old Testament, thinking it is not pertinent today.

Rest: It's a Matter of Obedience

In the Ten Commandments, taking a day of rest is listed as number four. Why is this commandment so prominently listed? Because when we take one day out of seven to rest we are saying, "I have faith in God." I trust that those things left undone, appointments missed, the money left unearned, etc., are in His hands and I will trust Him with the results. Think of it, the Designer of human beings, when giving His top ten rules, places at number four: Rest. He knows what He is doing.

When I was a boy growing up in Massachusetts, there was virtually no business conducted on Sundays. If you needed milk or bread, you'd better think ahead and get it on Saturday. Those were the days when the church and the Ten Commandments still had some influence in the laws and the way people lived. I am hopeful for the day when these things will be true again in our land.

Technically, the Sabbath is Saturday. In Genesis, we read of creation and each day that passes we read, "And there was evening, and there was morning—the first day," then "the second day," and so on through the sixth day. Because of this wording, the Jews and others have always considered a day to start at sundown and end at the next sundown. Even today, this is their practice and belief. Most others simply use midnight to mark the passing into a new day.

The Church (for the most part) worships on Sundays because it is the day Christ rose from the dead. Paul makes it clear that the specific day of the week is not the issue. In other words, going to church on Sunday does not mean you are keeping the Sabbath.

In the above text, the Pharisees complained (imagine that) to Jesus about His apparent disregard for the Sabbath because His disciples picked grain on that day as they walked through the field. Jesus pointed out that their interpretation and understanding of the Sabbath was skewed (Mark 2:23–28).

In Genesis when God finished with all His work, "He rested." I've always thought this was odd. God needs nothing. He does not grow weary. He is infinite in power, so creating the entire universe and every living thing did not even budge the needle on His power gauge. After all He did, the gauge still read, "Omnipotent." Yet He rested. Then I realized His reason for resting is found here in Jesus's statement: "The Sabbath was made for man." God, in His infinite wisdom and goodness, was taking a day off *for us*. My conclusion is that rest is a good gift from a good God. Rather than making it a burden as the Pharisees had done, God wants it to be a blessing.

When we read the Bible and a word like Sabbath comes up, we tend to either just glaze over it or attach a load of religious baggage to it. The word Sabbath simply means "to cease from labor." As the Jews began to develop synagogues, the Sabbath became a day of worship for them as well. Sometime during the intertestamental period (About 450 BC to 0 BC), the Jewish rabbis had added thirty-nine classes of prohibited actions for the Sabbath day.[11]

Apart from His claim to be the Messiah, there is no subject that caused more consternation among the Jewish leaders than this of Sabbath keeping. Isn't that just like humans to take something as simple as a day for rest—to take a beautiful gift from God—and corrupt it so that it becomes a burden instead? Some people, even today, seem to take the same approach. They are so dogmatic that the day of rest should be Saturday, they distort the gracious nature of God to be something Jesus contends against.

While in Bible College, I had to do some laundry and hauled my three to four weeks worth of clothes to a local laundromat. I loaded my clothes into the washers, inserted the necessary coins, and found a seat nearby. As I waited for my clothes to wash, I looked beside me to a table with some literature. One piece caught my eye. It was about the size of a *Reader's Digest* but thinner. I picked it up, and, as I began to read, recognized that it was about God and the Bible.

There was a true story written by a woman who remembered something that happened to her as a young girl. I got the impression that it was about a time in the mid-1900s. Apparently, she received some new, beautiful material and her mother was sewing a new dress for her to wear to church the next day. At one point, as the mother is working feverishly on the dress and is nearly done, she tells her daughter to go out on the porch and watch for the sunset. Now at this point in the story, I am beginning to think this is getting strange to me. Sure enough, the girl kept her watch on the sunset, and the moment she saw the sun dip below the horizon, she called out to her mother, who immediately stopped sewing, leaving the dress unfinished. The author went on to explain that as hard as that was for her as a little girl to deal with the disappointment of not having the new dress to wear, it had to be so because the Sabbath had to be kept.

When I got to that point in the story, I threw the booklet down, and in my heart I said, "That is not the God I serve!" I was angry because this little girl did not get her new dress. It seemed absurd to me. I had only known the Lord about five years and had only been through my first year of Bible school, but what I knew about the nature of God would not allow me to conceive of Him expecting this girl to go without a dress because the sun had gone down. What kind of good Father would want His daughter to miss out on something that would bring her so much delight? I believe wholeheartedly that God would have wanted that girl to have her beautiful, new dress to wear to church. The words of the Lord Jesus rang in my head, "The Sabbath was made for man, *not man for the Sabbath.*"

The worst thing we can do when we hear a story like that is have a knee-jerk reaction and think that the Sabbath is meaningless or that God didn't really intend for us to keep it. Many believers today break this commandment of God all the time.

One person considers one day more sacred

than another; another considers every day alike. Each of them should be fully convinced in their own mind. Whoever regards one day as special does so to the Lord. (Romans 14:5–6)

In our modern world it is unrealistic to expect that everyone could take the same day off. If our house caught on fire on a Saturday, I doubt there are any of us who would not call 911 because it *should be* a day of rest for everyone, including the firemen and police. The absolutist must reason that no one should be working because God commanded a certain day of rest. Let's be even more absurd. Wouldn't it be causing another to sin to flip on a light switch in our homes on the Sabbath? Isn't doing so causing someone else to have to work at a power plant or dam somewhere? I am certainly glad my electricity works seven days a week. Though many believers regard Sunday as their day of rest, I am a pastor and I can tell you most certainly, Sunday is no day of rest for me. In fact, it is the most intense and draining day of the week in my work.

Even though, in the New Testament, there is freedom about when to take the day of rest, it is disturbing how lightly believers take the idea of Sabbath. The other commandments we tend to take very seriously. We would not think lying or murdering or committing adultery or bowing down to idols would be okay, yet we are lax about keeping a day of rest. The Lord is a gracious God, but He is a God who expects His commandments to be obeyed not in a "letter of the Law" motif but in the "spirit of the Law." Some might think I sound legalistic here. I am not talking about legalism but obedience— not obedience to prove I love God but obedience that flows out of my love for Him and an understanding of His love for me.

Sabbath has more implication than just a day per week. We see in the Old Testament that there were also other kinds of Sabbaths. For instance, the Jews were to plant their fields for six years but let the land rest for the seventh. Servants who had worked for their masters were to be freed after six years as a kind of Sabbath. When the people of God came into the Promised Land, He commanded they take their times of rest, but they rebelled. Many times they worked seven days a week and did not rest the land. God had even prescribed that after forty-nine years (seven sets of seven), the next year, the fiftieth, was to be a special year called *Jubilee*. In the Year of Jubilee, slaves were to be freed and lands that had been put up as collateral were to be given back to the original owners. They were not to plant any crops that year because God promised they would be able to live off of the land the fiftieth year.

This would take some serious faith to pull off. As far as I can see from my study of the Bible, Israel never celebrated a year of Jubilee. In fact, it seems that they were not celebrating any of the Sabbath years God had commanded them to. After hundreds of years of disobedience toward God in this area and others, the king of Babylon, Nebuchadnezzar, came and overthrew Jerusalem, carrying the people off to captivity. At that time, Jeremiah the prophet spoke these words:

> He carried into exile to Babylon the remnant, who escaped from the sword, and they became servants to him and his successors until the kingdom of Persia came to power. The land enjoyed its sabbath rests; all the time of its desolation it rested, until the seventy years were completed in fulfillment of the word of the LORD spoken by Jeremiah. (2 Chronicles 36:20–21)

The people had not rested the land as they had been commanded. It took seventy years for the land to be "paid back" the Sabbaths that should have been kept. I can't help but wonder if, by way of principle, we are doing the same thing to ourselves when we don't rest properly. Could it be we are bringing trouble upon ourselves by not accepting the gift of rest God has offered? Please don't misunderstand me to imply God is punishing us for not taking Sabbaths, but we are bringing the trouble by failing to observe it just as we would experience injury if we jumped off a three-story building. The injury is not God's punishment. It is us reaping the pain of what we have sown by our foolishness of not observing the law of gravity.

Rest: It's a Matter of Faith

Remember in Mark 2, Jesus is with his disciples as they walked through the grainfields picking grain on the Sabbath. Do you think it is a coincidence that Jesus allows His disciples do these kinds of things on the Sabbath? If the Lord was really hungry and needed food for His disciples, I am certain there are many ways He could have come up with some groceries and not caused a stink with the Pharisees. I seem to remember a couple of stories about bread and fish for thousands working out pretty well. The very next story in Mark is one of Jesus healing a man in the synagogue on the Sabbath. He deliberately does these things on the Sabbath because it is essential that people understand the truth about the Law and grace. Without grace, we cannot be saved.

> For it is by grace you have been saved, through faith—and this is not from yourselves, it is the gift of God—not by works, so that no one can boast. (Ephesians 2:8–9)

Since it is by grace we are saved, then it is very important to understand what grace is and how to appropriate it to our lives. Grace is available by faith and is a gift of God. Grace is not from ourselves or procured by works. The pharisaical mindset saw Sabbath keeping as something you do to gain or earn salvation. If this thinking were allowed to perpetuate we would not be able to understand how to receive the gift of salvation by grace. The very reason Jesus came (to seek and save the lost) would have been destroyed. It was no accident that Jesus was in that grainfield and that He healed people on the Sabbath. It is essential for us to have a proper understanding of the place of the Law of God as a pattern and guideline for living—given for our good—but not the means of salvation.

This is what separates Christianity from the religions of the world. Other religions have doctrines of an incarnation, some even have stories of a resurrection, but the thing that makes Christianity unique is grace. "The notion of God's love coming to us free of charge, no strings attached, seems to go against every instinct of humanity. The Buddhist eight-fold path, the Hindu doctrine of karma, the Jewish covenant, and Muslim code of law—each of these offers a way to earn approval. Only Christianity dares to make God's love unconditional."[12]

The Pharisees had it backwards. They saw man as being made for the Sabbath rather than what God intended: The Sabbath was made for man. This not only frees up one day a week for rest and rejuvenation but it frees up the other six as we understand that we are the focus of God's creation and He is passionate about us.

We need to take appropriate time off. Certainly we are not under law but under grace, however, we rob ourselves and others when we do not practice the principles that are in God's Law.

Some people regularly work seven days a week. This may seem to be an honorable thing to do to provide for your family, but I challenge you to consider the cost to your health and the welfare of your family. Take a day off. Take a vacation. Rejuvenate, recreate, rest, and enjoy the life God has given you. If you have the kind of job that suggests or even requires sabbatical leaves, be sure to take them.

As a principle for a healthy life for ourselves, our families, and others around us, we need to take time to rest. It is like trusting God with a tenth of our money each month—He makes the 90 percent go further. We must also trust Him with the seventh of our time. He will make the remaining 86 percent more efficient, and I personally believe this will extend our lives and the quality of our lives for the future.

Finally, it says in Hebrews 4:9–11, "There remains, then, a Sabbath-rest for the people of God; for anyone who enters God's rest also rests from His own work, just as God did from His. Let us, therefore, make every effort to enter that rest." The ultimate Sabbath is in Christ. We rest from our own labors, our own works, and we enter into Christ by the grace of God, and so we rest in Christ.

For Pastors (and Those Who Love Their Pastors): Sabbaticals for Pastors

I was handed a book titled *Replenish* by Lance Witt some time ago and began to read it. I did not get very far into the book before I came across these statistics:

- 1,500 pastors leave the ministry permanently each month in America.
- 80 percent of pastors and 85 percent of their spouses feel discouraged in their roles
- 70 percent of pastors do not have a close friend, confidant, or mentor.
- Over 50 percent of pastors are so discouraged they would leave the ministry if they could but have no other way of making a living.
- Over 50 percent of pastors' wives feel that their husbands entering the ministry was the most destructive thing to ever happen to their families.
- 71 percent of pastors stated that they were burned out, and they battle fatigue on a weekly and even a daily basis.
- Only one out of ten ministers will actually retire as a minister.[13]

When I read those statistics I was shaken. What kind of

profession is this? Why are pastors failing and burning out? I went to a men's conference recently where Stu Webber, author of *Tender Warrior: God's Intention for a Man,* spoke. He addressed some of the unique pressures pastors face. He said, "Pastoring is a job that never goes away." I knew exactly what he meant by that. There is a sense in which a pastor are always on. Here are some examples:

A pastor must be an educator/teacher of the Word. People expect pastors to preach the finest messages in town. When one weekend's message is completed, it's time to start work on the next one. Wayne Cordeiro wrote: "One pastor told me it is like giving birth on Sunday, and then on Monday you find out you're pregnant again!"[14]

A pastor must be a visionary and leader. There is a mostly unspoken expectation that pastors hear clearly from God in every part of their lives and always know exactly what to do.

A pastor must be business oriented. We are blessed in our day to have buildings to assemble in, but along with facilities and properties come many responsibilities and challenges. We also live in a litigious age where we constantly have to think about avoiding lawsuits through proper policy and procedure.

A pastor must provide care for people (counseling). "A crisis is always just one phone call away."[15] There are staff, outreach, missions, business meetings, visitation, hospital calls, weddings, funerals, and every one of these facets of ministry has the potential of one or more people needing pastoral care.

A tremendous amount of what a pastor does is behind the scenes. Most of the church will only see the part on Sunday, which has led some people to think pastors only work one day a week. I don't know of any pastor who ever feels like he gets to a point where the job is done or that he gets to clock out.

This leads some of us to be critical of ourselves and push ourselves, not to mention that when you become a pastor you are painting a large target on yourself (or perhaps God has painted it on you). It is remarkable how many people will so quickly and easily take out their frustrations on a pastor. They can drop an email bomb on you so painful you feel like you would rather fall on a live hand grenade. I think we forget that pastors are just people, people who happen to have a call on their lives to serve and lay down their lives for a group of believers—just shepherds serving the Great Shepherd of the flock and trying to be a sheep themselves. Listen to the apostle Paul here in 2 Corinthians 11:23–29.

> I have worked much harder, been in prison more frequently, been flogged more severely, and been exposed to death again and again. Five times I received from the Jews the forty lashes minus one. Three times I was beaten with rods, once I was pelted with stones, three times I was shipwrecked, I spent a night and a day in the open sea, I have been constantly on the move. I have been in danger from rivers, in danger from bandits, in danger from my fellow Jews, in danger from Gentiles; in danger in the city, in danger in the country, in danger at sea; and in danger from false believers. I have labored and toiled and have often gone without sleep; I have known hunger and thirst and have often gone without food; I have been cold and naked. *Besides everything else, I face daily the pressure of my concern for all the churches* (emphasis mine).

I can't prove it but I almost feel like Paul is saying, I would rather be beaten than face the daily pressure of my concern for the Church. But, praise God, His grace is truly sufficient through the most difficult of times. I don't want to sound whiney or act like the life of a pastor is so much harder than anyone else's. That is not the point. But ministry has a unique set of dynamics to it that is hard to explain until you are in the middle of it. Even at times when things seem to be going extraordinarily well, there can be a very real sense of depletion. An example from the Bible would be the Prophet Elijah. In 1 Kings 18, he was at the top of his game so to speak. Fire had just fallen from heaven. The prophets of Baal had been put to death. The long drought was finally over, and the next thing you know Elijah is despondent and wiped out.

> He came to a broom bush, sat down under it and prayed that he might die. "I have had enough, LORD," he said. "Take my life; I am no better than my ancestors." Then he lay down under the bush and fell asleep. (1 Kings 19:4–5)

This kind of hopelessness seems crazy when he just called down fire from heaven, but I have spoken with many pastors who describe similar feelings on Mondays, when the weekend is over. It took Elijah forty days of being alone with God in the desert to finally have hope again and return to his ministry as a prophet. Times of rest and refreshing are absolutely imperative to the ministry.

Wayne Cordeiro is the pastor of New Hope Christian Fellowship, a church of over 20,000 people in Honolulu. A few years back he had a very serious breakdown. He wrote, "Finally it came to a head while I was out on a run on that balmy California evening. One minute I was jogging along on the sidewalk, and the next minute I was sitting on the curb, sobbing uncontrollably. I couldn't stop, and I didn't have a clue what was happening to me."[16]

In his book *Leading on Empty*, Wayne drives home the point that no one should push themselves to the point of breakdown like this before they stop and recharge their spiritual and emotional batteries. Pastors should absolutely take at least one day a week to rest and disconnect from the church. Pastors should take a reasonable amount of vacation time every year and, again, disconnect from the emails, cell phones, and even social media. Facebook and other social media have become an incredible way for pastors to keep in touch with people in the church, but there is a danger in checking your Facebook page on your day off because you will pick up the burdens of the people and never feel rested.

Pastors should take sabbatical leaves after several years of ministry or before the feelings and signs of burnout are present. The Lord Jesus told Peter that He would build *His* Church. You can trust the Lord with *His* Church while you are resting for a day, a week, or even months. Have faith in the Lord and believe in the people you pastor to hold up arms that are weak. In exercising faith to rest and get replenished, I believe we are doing what pleases God.

Chapter Ten
Faith to Worship

In July of 2000, we were four months into starting Praise Center as we met in the Grant Elementary School gymnasium that Sunday morning. The gym was huge and hollow. A bold sign on the wall said, "Seating Capacity 999." The sign seemed to really be mocking me that particular sunny summer day in July.

Back on April 2nd of that year, our first service in that room was attended by a total of twenty-one persons. Five of those were my family, but sixteen others actually showed up. I thought that was a great start for a baby church. Our house in Ellensburg had not sold yet, so every Sunday we would get up early, wake our three boys, load our Dodge Grand Caravan completely full of sound equipment and instruments—everything we needed to hold a service—and drive seventy-two miles to set up and be ready for a 10:00 a.m. service.

We would set up all the equipment and do a worship run-through at about 9:00 a.m. The good news for us was: I played acoustic guitar and led worship; Rhonda played keyboards and sang as well; Andrew, who was twelve at the time, played electric guitar very well; and Alex was a great drummer even at age ten. Abraham, our youngest, was only five at the time, and most Sundays was one of three kids in Children's Church. A college-aged student was learning to play bass guitar and was doing a pretty good job. All in all, for a tiny little church, we had a really full and great sounding worship band.

But now four months had passed and we were averaging about the same attendance every weekend. My wife is a woman of faith and a great ministry partner, but I could see it in her eyes each week. Those beautiful blue-greens would say, "Why are we doing this? Why am I leaving my home and friends?" I'll admit things had gotten off to a much slower start than I expected.

Then, on that sunny day, as usual we made the drive, set up, practiced, and got ready for the people to arrive. (I think most pastors will admit that extremes in weather on Sundays can really be a bummer. If it is miserable out, stormy or snowy, we think, *Nobody will come today because of the weather.* On the other hand, if the weather is too nice, we think, *Nobody will come today because of the weather.*)

As ten o'clock arrived, we started singing. There we were, five of us, our full band, up front playing in a room that could seat 999 people, but there were only four people in the seats (including my five-year-old). I was leading worship with my eyes closed. I couldn't stand looking at what amounted to really only three people who actually didn't have to be there because their parents made them come. I thought, *Why are we doing this?* On the outside I was smiling and singing praise songs, but on the inside I was complaining to God. I was thinking of the children of Israel in the wilderness saying, "Have You brought us out here to die?"

In that moment of conflict and complaint I heard the Lord speak to my heart and say to me, "Sal, I brought you here to this valley to worship Me. If you are worshipping, you are obeying Me." Immediately following, I also felt the Lord encourage me with the same words He had spoken to Peter, "I will build My Church."

Suddenly, the weight of that moment lifted off of me. I had been trying so hard to build this new church, and now, clearly, Jesus was inviting me to hand Him my heavy burden in order to receive one from Him that was easy and light. I accepted that invitation and felt released from anyone's expectations except His. Freeing! I stood there, now worshipping without complaining, and lifting praise to God by faith, trusting that my obedience to Him would result in Him blessing me, my family, and Praise Center.

Earnestly Seek God

Faith is at the very heart of worship. It takes faith to worship an invisible God. Now, of course, if we could see God faith wouldn't be needed anymore. However, we would not be able to please Him because, remember, "without faith it is impossible to please God." But we must continue reading this verse: "because anyone who comes to him must *believe that he exists* (emphasis mine) and that He rewards those who earnestly seek him" (Hebrews 11:6). *Believing that He exists is faith.* The words for believe and faith are used interchangeably in the New Testament and are generally forms of the same Greek word. Looking at this verse again, we see it is impossible to please God without faith, and faith starts with belief in the existence of God. What this chapter is about is the next phrase in the verse: "He rewards those who earnestly seek him."

What does it mean to *earnestly seek* God? Primarily it means to worship Him. The first verse of this same chapter reads, "Now faith is confidence in what we hope for and assurance about what we do not see." The writer of Hebrews continues to talk about faith throughout the entire chapter.

At the beginning of chapter 12, we see the word "therefore." One of my instructors in Bible College said, "Whenever you see a 'therefore' look and see what it is *there* for." Therefore is a bridge between what was just said to what is about to be said. There are three times the word *therefore* is used in chapter 12. Each one builds upon what was mentioned previously until we come to the apex found in the final verse of the chapter and the final *therefore*: "Therefore, since we are receiving a kingdom that cannot be shaken, let us be thankful, and so worship God acceptably with reverence and awe, for our 'God is a consuming fire'" (Hebrews 12:28–29). "Worship God acceptably with reverence and awe!" This is where faith is leading us. This is what faith is all about. This is the object of our faith. Having faith in faith itself is an endless and fruitless pursuit. God is the object of our faith. Our faith is in Him and our ultimate goal is to worship Him.

With this in mind, I want to look again at Abraham's life, where we see faith and worship converge in one incredible moment.

> Some time later God tested Abraham. He said to him, "Abraham!" "Here I am," he replied. Then God said, "Take your son, your only son, whom you love—Isaac—and go to the region of Moriah. Sacrifice him there as a burnt offering on a mountain I will show you." Early the next morning Abraham got up and loaded his donkey. He took with him two of his servants and his son Isaac. When he had cut enough wood for the burnt offering, he set out for the place God had told him about. On the third day Abraham looked up and saw the place in the distance. He said to his servants, "Stay here with the donkey while I and the boy go over there. We will worship and then we will come back to you." (Genesis 22:1–5)

In verse 5 we have the first mention of the word "worship" in our English Bibles. In the discipline of Bible study, someone has coined the phrase, "Law of first mention." The idea behind this is to pay attention to the first time a word or idea is brought up in Scripture because it may set the stage for further understanding as we progress through the Word. Although the word "worship" appears here for the first time in English, the word for worship in the original Hebrew (s*hawkaw*) is first used a little earlier in the Bible, in Genesis 18:2. This describes an occasion in Abraham's life as well.

The LORD appeared to Abraham near the great

trees of Mamre while he was sitting at the entrance to his tent in the heat of the day. Abraham looked up and saw three men standing nearby. When he saw them, he hurried from the entrance of his tent to meet them and bowed low to the ground. (Genesis 18:1–2)

The words "bowed low" are translated from the same word as worship in chapter 22. Abraham is certainly known for his faith, but he was also a committed worshipper of God. Even though in other instances the word *shawkaw* may not be used specifically, we find that worship is found in various forms throughout the life of Abraham from the very beginning. Consider:

- He built an altar there to the LORD, who had appeared to him. (Genesis 12:7)
- From the Negev he went from place to place until he came . . . to the place . . . where he had first built an altar. There Abram called on the name of the LORD. (Genesis 13:3–4)
- He built an altar to the LORD. (Genesis 13:18)
- (When the LORD appeared to him) Abram fell facedown. (Genesis 17:1–3)
- Abraham giving a tenth as an offering to Melchizedek could be seen as an act of worship. (Genesis 14:18–20)
- When the three visitors come to him they appear as men, but two of them are angels and the other is the LORD Himself. Abraham recognizes this and prepares a meal for them. This is a form of worship. (Genesis 18:1–8)

Abraham as a worshipper is also a model of prayer.

- He interceded for the people of Sodom and Gomorrah and for his nephew Lot. (Genesis 18:22–33)

- Later, he prayed for King Abimelech, Abimelech's wife, and their people, and God healed them. (Genesis 20:17–18)

We need to see worship as more than just bowing down to God. Worship includes living lives of holiness, prayer, giving, sacrifice, and faith. Worship is not simply the act of singing, lifting hands, kneeling, and praying. It is also serving meals, holding children, doing a job as unto the Lord, or doing schoolwork as unto the Lord. These can all be done as worship, and Abraham excelled at living that way. He lived a life of worship to God.

Receive Hope through Worship

I don't know of any decent father who wouldn't give up his own life for any one of his children. Abraham was no different. What I want us to see most of all is, from Abraham's perspective, he planned to kill his son and offer him to God as a burnt offering and he called this supreme sacrifice *worship!* He said to his servants, "We will go over there. We will worship, and we will come back to you." Notice he said, "*We* will come back." Hebrews 11:19 tells us that "Abraham reasoned that God could even raise the dead." Somehow he figured it would work out and God would not forsake His promise. He had hope in the outcome because he knew God and trusted His promises. Part of worshipping God is found in the form of passing tests we are given by God. By facing these challenges in the right way, we show our faith, and our faith becomes worship to God.

It seems to me that all great promises from God go through a cycle of life, death, and life again. Even the promise of a Savior to the world went through this cycle. Many of us have been through this cycle in our own lives on one or more occasions.

In the late seventies, while living in Portland, I met a man who used to race motorcycles. When he gave his life to the Lord, he felt that God was asking him to give up motorcycles completely. He willingly "died" to motorcycles and was prepared to do so for the rest of his life. But, after a few years, he felt that God released him to get a motorcycle again because it was no longer an idol to him.

What if God were to tell us to give up the thing we think is most important—in essence, to do what Abraham did and be willing to put it to death. Are we ready to do it? Right now we may feel as though we are in the middle of that death cycle of laying things down. We may feel that our finances are dead. We may feel that our marriage is dead. We may feel that our career is dead. There are things we hope for and dream about—things we would like to do or places we would like to go. Somewhere deep in our souls we understand that God is calling us to a radical faith that says give it to Him. He is saying, "Trust Me with it and lay it down." And if is supposed to be given back to us, God can take the thing we give as a sacrifice and raise it back up again.

Our God can take things that have no life and bring life from the dead. He did it literally with several people in the Bible. He did it with His only Son, and He will do it with us. Ultimately it is our hope in the Resurrection that is the greatest promise of all. Where are we in the process of our faith? Are we living life as worshippers of God? Are we passing the tests that come along in life? Are we facing the death of a dream knowing that we may face several cycles of these things?

Continuing with the theme of worship, I want to examine two familiar stories that might help us to see how faith and worship work together in practical terms in our lives. It takes faith to worship—in spite of the enemy's attack, in spite of the conditions we find ourselves in, and in spite of what it costs us. Seeing our sacrifice to God as worship releases hope in us of the power of resurrection.

Receive Victory through Worship

There are times when we feel overwhelmed by things that are coming against us.

- Perhaps the bills are piling up and the washing machine stopped working or the car needs a new transmission.
- Perhaps we have had a bad week at work and we come home to some problem at home.
- Perhaps we have a dispute with someone at work or at school and it seems to snowball out of control.
- Perhaps we have given in to some substance or to a sinful thought pattern that seems to be taking over our lives.
- Perhaps some medical or physical condition has come and is poised to, at the very least, steal our joy or, at the most, our lives.

Everybody faces battles in their lives of one sort or another. The question is, what are we going to do about it? Who are we going to call upon? Who cares enough about us to come to our aid when we are facing a battle? The story of King Jehoshaphat, from 2 Chronicles 20, is well known and illustrates the power of faith through worship better than perhaps any other. Three nations joined forces to create a "vast army." Their intent was to attack the people of God, to destroy them, and literally drive them out of the land. Jehoshaphat's response was to pray and fast. In fact, he led all the people to come together and to *earnestly seek* the Lord. And together they came from all parts of Judah. The men and their wives, their children, and even the little ones, stood before the Lord.

After this time of prayer and fasting, the Spirit of the Lord came upon a prophet named Jahaziel. The prophet spoke these words: "Do not be afraid or discouraged because of this vast army. For the battle is not yours, but God's" (2 Chronicles 20:15). This was all Jehoshaphat needed to hear. With faith now rising in his heart, he stood before the people and said, "Listen to me, Judah and people of Jerusalem! Have faith in the LORD your God and you will be upheld; have faith in his prophets and you will be successful" (2 Chronicles 20:20–21). Notice the word faith here. Have faith in God and have faith in what God says.

With faith in their hearts they went out to face the enemy, and, as they went, Jehoshaphat gave further instructions. He asked for the singers. He called for the choir. I don't mean to stereotype here, but when I went to high school the boys who were in the choir were generally not the same ones who played football. As an outside observer, someone might think a screw had come loose in the king's head. When you go to war you want the meanest, toughest guys you can get. But Jehoshaphat clearly believed what had been spoken: *The battle is the Lord's.*

These singers went out ahead of the rest of the army and sang a refrain, some form of which is found several times in the Old Testament—something we ought to learn to sing ourselves when faced with adversity.

"Give thanks to the LORD,
for his love endures forever."

With their eyes and hearts on the Lord rather than the approaching troubles, they walked on confidently toward the battle. Early in the morning they began their march and with it their song. God caused great confusion to come upon the enemy armies so they all began to attack each other. The attack was so intense and the disorder was so great that every single soldier in the whole army was ultimately killed. By the time the singers, still singing their song, came over the crest of the last hill to look into the valley below, all they saw were dead bodies. It took the Israelites three days to recover all the plunder— every thing that was of value—from the dead. On the fourth day, they all got together in a nearby valley called Beracah. Beracah means praise. They praised God going into the battle, and they praised God coming out.

Are there battles we are facing?

137

How are we going to deal with them?
What if, instead of worrying, we worshipped!
What if, instead of panicking, we praised!

If we think about this and decide it sounds ridiculous, it is because we lack faith.

- It takes faith to sing, "Give thanks to the Lord," when there doesn't seem to be much to be thankful for.
- It takes faith to sing, "The Lord is good," when bad things are happening.
- It takes faith to sing, "His love endures forever," when difficulties we face cause us to feel unsure of His care.

What do we have to lose? What do we stand to gain? The next time we face something tough, we should worship Him ahead of that battle. In fact, why not put this book down for a moment and worship Him now! I expect we will see that we will begin to experience victory as we do so.

Receive Freedom through Worship

In Acts 16 we come to one of the most remarkable stories in the New Testament. Here we find the account of two men who have been severely beaten, imprisoned, and locked into stocks, which likely spread their legs apart to the point of severe discomfort. It is late and most of the other prisoners are probably trying to get some sleep. But something is going on in cell block D. There is a sound you don't usually hear in such a place. Is it singing we hear? "About midnight Paul and Silas were praying and singing hymns to God, and the other prisoners were listening to them" (Acts 16:25).

We think if we suffer in any way or if something seems to go against what we perceive God's plan to be, we must have missed God somehow. To the contrary, it is many times through our suffering that God gets even greater glory. Paul and Silas were not singing to get something from God, they were singing to give God the praise that belongs to Him. God is not worthy of praise only when things are going well. He is worthy of praise at all times. In the middle of their troubles and suffering they sang.

Their singing got God's attention, and the next thing you know . . . "Suddenly there was such a violent earthquake that the foundations of the prison were shaken. At once all the prison doors flew open, and everyone's chains came loose" (Acts 16:26). What a great earthquake. It was so selective in its shaking that not only did it open *all* the prison doors of *every* prisoner but the chains on their feet and hands came loose as well! I love to watch certain commentators try to explain how a "natural" earthquake could have brought this about. It's not that this region of what is now Turkey is not prone to earthquakes, but consider the timing and the discriminating nature of this quake. Every stock and chain fell off. Every door opened. But no one was harmed by a collapse or any collateral damage. When God uses a natural thing at just the right time it becomes supernatural.

As believers, when we praise and worship God we are shaking things up. When the incredible name of Jesus is on our lips in song and worship, there is a rumbling going on in the spiritual realm. And when, in the face of our own personal pain, we can rise above it and call on the name of the Lord, we send forth tremors that shake free the prison doors and break chains from other people's lives as well. It wasn't just Paul and Silas who were freed but their praise opened the door for everyone. Everybody's chains came loose. Everybody! Even the people who were not praising, even the people who didn't know God, even the people who were sleeping. Everybody's chains came loose!

But what was good for the prisoners was not good for the guard. He was about to kill himself because if a Roman guard loses a prisoner he will be executed. Can you imagine this poor jailer? He had his sword in hand and was about to lean upon it and kill himself, when he heard Paul shout, "Don't harm yourself! We are all here!" Whew! No one had escaped.

The freedom that came to Paul, Silas, and the rest of the prisoners did not need to cost this man his life. When the jailer realized the gravity of the situation he cried out,

"Sirs, what must I do to be saved?" They replied, "Believe in the Lord Jesus, and you will be saved—you and your household" (Acts 16:30–31). What a relief for him: Being brought to the point of death caused him to, at that moment, evaluate his life. When he was spared, his first reaction was to seek salvation. The jailer was saved, his household was saved, and though the text doesn't state it, we have to imagine that the other prisoners and guards were brought to some point of decision because of what they had seen.

While we worship God in our homes and our churches, people of all ages get set free. Freedom is contagious. As we get free, we will take this freedom into our communities, and we are going to see entire households coming to Christ.

It takes faith to worship in spite of the things we see or don't see around us. As we exercise that faith in this way, we see incredible benefits from it. Earlier we read that God "rewards those who seek Him." The sacrifice of praise enables the *hope of resurrection life in us*. Worshipping through battles we face brings *victory in our lives*, and worshipping in times of trouble brings *freedom to us and others*. Great rewards, if you ask me, and such worship pleases God.

Chapter Eleven
The Word of Faith

Have you ever said something you wish you could take back? I suppose everyone has. Quite some time ago, a friend of mine went with his wife to a pastors' conference at large church in Southern California. As I remember the story, they had arrived early and were parked in a parking spot right next to a marked disabled parking stall. Apparently, my friend's wife, noticing how many designated places the parking lot had was thinking out loud and said, "I wonder how many people use those parking places who are not really disabled?"

As they were getting out of their car, someone drove up and parked in that very space beside them. A young man got out of the driver's seat very nimbly and started to walk toward the back of the car. My friend's wife thought he was heading toward the church building for the conference and said, "You don't look handicapped to me." The stunned young man said, "You should be more sensitive." With that, he opened up the trunk of his car to remove a wheelchair, which he opened and took to the passenger's side of the car to help his wife into the chair. Obviously, my friend's wife was mortified, but the damage was done. The words had been spoken, and there was no taking them back.

That is the problem with words. Once they are out there, they are out there. And the aggravating thing about it is, we can say nice things all day to a person (and we should) but one poor choice of words can erase a whole day of good ones. Can I hear an "amen" from all the married folks out there. How important are words? How much attention should we give to what we say? In the third chapter of James we have the most definitive passage on the importance of our words and speech. Let's let God's Word speak to us as we read this passage *aloud*.

> Not many of you should become teachers, my fellow believers, because you know that we who teach will be judged more strictly. We all stumble in many ways. Anyone who is never at fault in what they say is perfect, able to keep their whole body in check. When we put bits into the mouths of horses to make them obey us, we can turn the whole animal. Or take ships as an example. Although they are so large and are driven by strong winds, they are steered by a very small rudder wherever the pilot wants to go. Likewise, the tongue is a small part of the body, but it makes great boasts. Consider what a great forest is set on fire by a small spark. The tongue also is a fire, a world of evil among the parts of the body. It corrupts the whole body, sets the whole course of one's life on fire, and is itself set on fire by hell. All kinds of animals, birds, reptiles and sea creatures are being tamed and have been tamed by mankind, but no human being can tame the tongue. It is a restless evil, full of deadly poison. With the tongue we praise our Lord and Father, and with it we curse human beings, who have been made in God's likeness. Out of the same mouth come praise and cursing. My brothers and sisters, this should not be. Can both fresh water and salt water flow from the same spring? My brothers and sisters, can a fig tree bear olives, or a grapevine bear figs? Neither can a salt spring produce fresh water. (James 3:1–12)

We live in an area of Washington State that is prone to forest fires. The eastern slope of the Cascade Mountains gets considerably less precipitation than the western side does. People who don't know the topography of our area might hear I am from Washington and say with disdain, "It sure rains a lot there." What they don't realize is that our area gets only about nine inches of rainfall a year. This is great if you love sunshine and doing things outdoors. The downside is how dry our forests become in the summertime.

In early September of 2012, a lightning storm with little rainfall came through and started a fire that, despite the bravery and hard work of the firefighters, kept burning for about a month. The smoke hung in our valley the entire time, causing health concerns for many. So much smoke filled the air on some days that you couldn't see more than a couple of blocks away. Toward the end of the month, I heard a local weatherman on the radio say that if it weren't for this smoke we would have had the best weather on record for a September. He was adding insult to injury. It was miserable for everyone who lives here. All of it, in essence, was started by a spark.

In this text, James is saying that our words have the same effect in a spiritual way. It doesn't take much, but something we said that we shouldn't have may seem small to us yet the effects are far-reaching and devastating.

When it comes to the subject of faith, I don't suppose there is anything quite as important to consider as the words that come from our mouths. Words are inexorably linked to faith. There is importance in what we say *and* in what we *don't* say.

Watch What You Say

Back in 2008, our church purchased another building. Our congregation had grown to around five hundred in regular attendance on the weekend, and we were doing four services on Sundays in a building that could seat 150 people. Nearly every day I drove past an older building in our community that looked dilapidated. Almost every window had broken glass from rocks being thrown through them by vandals. The roofing was peeling off in places, and things were very rundown inside and out. We were able to purchase this building inexpensively, and our congregation did almost all of the remodeling. I like doing remodeling, and many times I would be at the building working and need something that was in the basement and have to carry it to the third or fourth floor. Oh, did I mention it has *four stories* of stairs?

> Stairs, stairs everywhere
> Stairs go up, stairs go down
> Sometimes stairs go round and round . . .

I felt like I was in a Dr. Seuss nightmare. So I started complaining about them. "Stupid stairs!" I was grumbling and began to get a bad attitude.

Then one day I felt encouraged by the Holy Spirit to modify my speech. The sense of His communication with me was that I had better change my words about those stairs because like it or not I was going to be climbing them every day. From that time on, every time I began to walk up the stairs, I started saying *out loud*, "I love these stairs; I love these stairs." At first I had to work at saying it, but after a while my attitude really started to change. I began to think of the stairs as healthy for me, and soon my attitude began to align with my new way of speaking. It used to be, if I go down, I will *have* to come up; but now it is, if I go down, I *get* to come up. This might sound a bit silly to you, but I am absolutely serious about it.

What would life be like if we started talking differently about things that are good for us but we don't like doing? For instance, what if someone who doesn't like reading began to speak out, "I love to read!" Or, what if someone who doesn't

144

like to exercise started saying, "I love exercise!" We can change the way we talk about all kinds of things, like housecleaning, yard work, saving money, school, where we live, our health, our financial state, and our vehicles. What else should we change our speech over?

- What are we saying about our jobs?
- What are we saying about our spouse?
- What are we saying about our kids?
- What are we saying about relationships?

In Romans 4:17 we read, "God who . . . calls into being things that were not." This is what we need to do as well. Call things that don't exist into being. For example, we need to change how we speak about our health. We are far too quick to speak diseases and afflictions into our lives. We sniff a little in the spring and announce loudly to all, "I have allergies!" Our throat gets a little sore in the fall and we proclaim boldly, "I have the flu!"

I think we accept sickness sometimes. Occasionally, it seems, people verbalize ill health because they want attention. You know, when we were children if we were sick, normally our moms or dads would let us stay in our pajamas all day and cover us up with a warm blanket and lay a cool washcloth on our foreheads. They would sit by us and bring us things to drink and eat. And, if our parents were cool, we got to watch cartoons all day instead of going to school. Let's face it, when we were little and sick we got treated like kings and queens.

Now we are all grown up, but we get a little selfish and want some attention. If we feel a little something we say, "I'm sick!" The truth is, we may feel a bit ill and we are perfectly able to go to work or church, but we would rather sit around in our pajamas watching cartoons (or football). First of all, we just need to grow up; but most of all, we need to stop confessing sickness over our lives. It should sound more like this, "I have a sore throat, but I am thanking God for good health today." Instead of complaining about aches and pains we should say, "Thank You, Lord, for healing my body and giving me strength. We are changing our speech. We are speaking life and health and peace over our lives.

This leads me to my second point.

Break the Power of Curses

After drilling his platoon in the hot sun, the sergeant barked out a final order: "All right, you idiots, fall out! The men dispersed, but one private stood firm. The sergeant glared as the private smiled and said, "There sure were a lot of them weren't there, Sergeant?"

If we say things long enough or we hear others say them enough we will begin to believe them. But it is worse than that: There really is power in our words so that it is not just a matter of starting to believe something, but our words can actually add fuel to the fire of hell to work in our lives and the lives of others we may be speaking about. With our words we can speak things into existence. Proverbs 18:21 says "The tongue has the power of life and death." Do we grasp the implications of this verse? What comes out of our mouths has the power to bring life and it has the power to bring death. What will we choose to do?

Many of us grew up in homes where these kinds of curses were spoken—where harsh or thoughtless words have been verbalized over our lives. Some might be in those homes even now. We may have been called stupid or a failure. Perhaps a parent or a relative made degrading comments to us about our physical appearance and, since then, we have seen ourselves through that lens. This can be a curse. We may have had a past employer who berated us and spoke of inadequacy or inability and we have lived with that curse. Someone, maybe even a well-meaning doctor, may have made a comment about our lack of health in an area (example: "You sound like you have asthma"). Those words settled into our souls, and then we began to speak them as well.

Be careful when others speak over you words that start with "you'll never" or "you can't" or "you always." And, for heaven's sake, don't be guilty of saying these things yourself. Be careful not to speak over your own life things like: "Why does this *always* happen to me?" "I *always* seem to get sick." "All the men in my family die young." "Alcoholism runs in our family." "We have heart conditions." All of these are examples of words having the power of death in them.

Some people are very concerned about family medical history. Now, I totally understand the reason for this and I am not denying the science of biology. Genetics and other factors certainly can play a part in our health. Everyone will need to decide what family health history he or she needs to know or not know, but for myself, I feel it would be best for me to not know about these things because I don't really want to give any power to that disease or health issue in my life. Someone might tell me that I am living in denial. To which I would reply, "Of course, I am." Didn't Jesus tell us to deny ourselves? I think denying ourselves has broader ramifications than just denying our fleshly appetites.

The Lord is my healer. I really believe I am a new creation. Second Corinthians 5:17 says, "Therefore, if anyone is in Christ, the new creation has come: The old has gone, the new is here!" Family curses of all kinds are broken in Jesus's name. Even in spite of the fact that my mother was a believer, she used to say, "I won't live to see grandchildren grow up." She died at sixty-two years young and lived a life of often speaking the worst about her health: *my* asthma, *my* heart problems, and *my* condition. Years ago Rhonda used to say to the kids, "You're going to drive me crazy." I asked her to stop saying that. I don't want a crazy wife unless she's crazy about me.

Since the economic downturn began in 2008, I have been talking about our church's finances and on occasion telling others how bad they have been. Recently, I felt the Lord chastise me for continuing to confess that. It is time to break that curse in the name of Jesus Christ! Since I changed how I spoke about the finances, in just two months we have seen a distinct turnaround. I am not saying that we are to be dishonest or that we do not let others know of needs. How else could we help each other unless we knew what to do? But I feel like God is telling me to break the curse of *lack* and begin to confess *plenty* in Jesus's name.

My wife and I like to golf. Golf can become an obsession for some people. Did you hear about the husband and wife who were on the ninth green when suddenly she collapsed from what seemed to be a heart attack! "Help me, dear," she groaned to her husband. The husband called 911 on his cell phone, talked for a few moments, and then picked up his putter and lined up his putt.

His wife raised her head off the green and stared at him. "I'm dying here and you're putting?"

"Don't worry, dear," said the husband calmly, "they found a doctor on the second hole and he's coming to help you."

"Well, how long will it take for him to get here?" she asked feebly.

"No time at all," said her husband. "Everybody's already agreed to let him play through."

Recently Rhonda and I were preparing to go golfing on Memorial Day, and I realized how busy the course was likely to be. It also dawned on me that we would likely be paired up with two other people to make a foursome. In my mind I thought about how embarrassed I was by my lack of skill, and I was preparing to say to these strangers something like, "I'm really bad at this game" or "I hope you don't mind playing with someone who stinks." One time someone asked me what my handicap was and I said, "Playing golf." Recently, as I was thinking this through, again I felt a prompting by the Spirit to stop confessing how badly I golf. This may seem juvenile to you, but I really like to play and I would like to be better at it. So I have stopped saying those things about my game. Even if my score doesn't improve, isn't a person with a good attitude better to golf with?

If we are not careful we may speak death and curses over ourselves. If we aren't paying attention, others may speak those things over us. What do we do in these cases? I love this verse from Proverbs 26:2, "Like a fluttering sparrow or a darting swallow, an undeserved curse does not come to rest." We don't have to allow those undeserved curses to stick to us. Just let them flutter and dart away! James said that both cursing and blessing or praise should not come from the same mouth. The power of praise and blessing is an untapped resource in the kingdom of God. So let's do it right. Let's begin to be a people who pronounce blessings by faith and speak praise!

Engage the Power of Blessings

Earlier I said we need to be careful what we say from a negative viewpoint so we do not speak death or curses over our lives or the lives of others. Stopping the harmful and damaging speech is important, but it is only half of the equation. In other words, *there are things that need to be spoken by us over our lives and over the lives of others that will bring wholeness, peace, salvation, and healing to them.* We have no idea how much power is in our tongue. Yes the power of a curse or death is in the tongue, but so is the power of life and blessings!

Our words have the power to bring life! There is power in our words to bring about good. Back when my youngest son, Abraham, was nine years old, he and I were watching *Star Wars: Attack of the Clones.* Matter-of-factly he said, "The force in *Star Wars* is nothing. They have to concentrate to move an object, and it looks like it takes a lot of effort. Jesus said all we have to do is *speak* to a mountain and it will be thrown into the sea." Wow! The faith of children! My son at nine was more discerning about faith than many adults I know. But, notice, we have to *speak* to that mountain, not just wish it or think about it.

Whenever my children showed some aptitude for something, I would purposefully speak over them blessings. If

I saw them show kindness to someone, I made it a point to remark, "You are really a kind person." If I saw them excel at some subject in school, I would say something like, "You are great at math." But taking it a step further, even if I saw something lacking in some area their lives, I would use it as an opportunity to speak about the potential that was in them to be great rather than focus on the negative. There is a propensity for parents to see some area of bad behavior or a failure of some kind and focus on that. A child can come home with a report card that has four A's and one C. We tend to talk about the "C" and say, "You really need to work on your math" or "What's going on in your English class?" Something tells me more emphasis on and accolades for the places they are excelling will result in more desire to do so in every area.

It also seems to me I hear a lot of parents speaking over their young children things like, "You are so beautiful" or "You are so handsome." This can certainly help their children's self-image, but I fear too much emphasis on things that have to do with looks can backfire. We should keep affirming our kids in these areas, but we should add to this (and even all the more emphasize) attributes of character or intelligence and spiritual growth.

So here's what I suggest. Start speaking blessings out loud over our own lives. Start speaking blessings over our family. Say good things about and to our friends. Start speaking blessings over our destiny. Speak blessings over our schools, our churches, and our nation. It is no wonder America is in such trouble when so many terrible things being said about her. The news media does a great job of speaking the negatives. As believers, we ought to speak blessings over our nation.

Let's start today to get in the habit of speaking the word of faith and blessings over others. If we catch ourselves calling someone a name or cutting them down, we should ask for forgiveness, turn it around, and speak a blessing instead. If we catch someone else speaking a curse over another, gently rebuke them and say: "Speak blessings!" If they won't change, don't worry because the "curse" is undeserved and will not stay.

We were created for worship and praise. The very best use of our voice is to lift it up in praise to bless our glorious King. As we speak the word of faith to God and praises to Him, we actually change the spiritual atmosphere around us, our homes, our churches, our schools, our communities, and our world. Here are three steps that will help us make those changes:

Step 1: Ask God to help us change our confession.
Step 2: Break the power of curses we or others have spoken by renouncing them.
Step 3: Replace those curses with words of blessings!

Speak by Faith

We can say we have great faith, but unless what we believe comes out of our mouths our faith cannot go to work. In considering how faith works together with what we say, look at this, "By faith we understand that the universe was formed at God's command, so that what is seen was not made out of what was visible" (Hebrews 11:3). I happen to believe that if God had wanted to He could have just simply *thought* the universe into existence and it would have appeared, but this is not what He did. He formed the universe with a spoken *command*.

In Genesis we read, God *said*, "Let there be light"; God *said*, "Let us make man in our image"; etc. In fact, in Genesis 1, God *speaks* nine different times. Why does He speak it? I believe it is for our sake, as an example to us, so that we will learn to speak the word of faith. The Bible tells us that: Faith comes by smelling. (No, that's not right.) Faith comes by tasting. (Wrong again.) Faith comes by touching. (Nope.) How about this? Faith comes by seeing. Absolutely not! If we see it, we don't need faith anymore. Faith is the evidence of things *not* seen. God *spoke* the universe into being as an example for us because faith comes by *hearing*. For us to hear something, it must be *spoken*. We can say we have faith for something, but if that faith never materializes into something that is spoken or done it is not faith at all.

Are we facing some health issue or financial crisis? Are we dealing with children who are rebellious or a relationship that is crumbling? It really matters what we say. It really matters what comes out of our mouths. If we can't even be saved without confessing or declaring (Romans 10:9), then what makes us think we can see anything supernatural if we don't exercise our faith by *speaking* God's truth and God's Word over the troubles we face? Go ahead! Start declaring. Start proclaiming. Start speaking out loud, "Let there be _____!" Rather than feeling regret over things we have said that we shouldn't have, imagine how delighted God is going to be as we learn to speak by faith.

Chapter Twelve
Live by Faith

One of the most important verses in my own life and, in my opinion, the Bible is found in Galatians 2:20. Circle, underline, and highlight this verse. Mark it and memorize it.

> "I have been crucified with Christ and I no longer live, but Christ lives in me. The life I live in the body, I live by faith in the Son of God, who loved me and gave himself for me."

The apostle Paul brings a savage thought into our minds with this opening phrase, "I have been crucified." It means co-crucified. Isn't that a lovely thought? Crucifixion is said to be one of the most torturous and wicked forms of capital punishment ever devised. We read about the cross, we sing about the cross, we praise God and thank Him for the cross, and along the way we tend to almost view the cross through rose-colored lenses. What I mean is, we have to see the cross for all that it signifies. It means death. It is brutal and bloody. Can you imagine how strange it would be to sing songs about hangings or lethal injections? Yet for us who have been saved by the work of Jesus on the cross, it *is* beautiful and glorious. What I am asking for is the ability to love the cross but not forget its deadly side.

When we come to Christ we are made new. Thankfully it isn't just a one-time opportunity, but every day there is a fresh set of mercies from God to become the new creation we were meant to be. Jesus told His disciples that if they wanted to follow Him they would have to take up their cross daily. The verb for crucified here is in the perfect tense, which means it is a past completed action having present finished result. What Jesus accomplished there, nearly two thousand years ago, is still as potent and real today as it was then. This being said, the cross has present implications for your life and mine—not only for salvation but for day-to-day living.

I No Longer Live

As a pastor I have many opportunities to perform wedding ceremonies. More often than not, the couple will have a time in the wedding where they light the unity candle. This is a beautiful and visual way to depict marriage. Two flames united to become one. The couples then blow out their individual candles as a sign of extinguishing their own lives in choosing to become one.

I have heard recently that some people are now leaving their individual candles lit to signify independence and personal freedom. Oh brother! If you want independence and personal freedom, don't get married! I also heard of one couple who had discussed these options with their pastor. The soon-to-be groom, after thinking about it, asked, "How about if we leave mine lit and blow out hers?" Someone is in for a rude awakening.

The unity candle can be an example of our life in Christ as well. Jesus was willing to have His flame extinguished by dying for us so that we could have the possibility of relationship with Him. However, for us to be in relationship with Him we have to extinguish our flame. The idea of independence and so-called personal freedom is the antithesis of what the Christian life is all about. He gave His life for us. We lay down our lives for Him, and, by God's grace, the two become one. It is the willingness to lay down our lives that Galatians 2:20 refers to when we say, "I no longer live." This is at the same time both disconcerting and comforting to us, isn't it?

The "me" I used to be was never the "me" I really wanted

to be anyway. Indeed, as I described in an earlier chapter, God gave me an opportunity to live a new life through Him. The old life had to go, and I am glad. Paul touches on this concept of dying to our old lives throughout his writings in the New Testament. Here we see the same theme being explored in the book of Romans. As you read this passage, notice the words died, death, buried, and dead.

> What shall we say, then? Shall we go on sinning so that grace may increase? By no means! We are those who have died to sin; how can we live in it any longer? Or don't you know that all of us who were baptized into Christ Jesus were baptized into his death? We were therefore buried with him through baptism into death in order that, just as Christ was raised from the dead through the glory of the Father, we too may live a new life. (Romans 6:1–4)

Now, since, according to this passage, we are truly dead, then, we have no more rights. Only the living have rights. We need to understand this. We get frustrated, irritated, and angry because we believe our *rights* have been violated. I had a man come into my office some time ago and tell me of how terrible his life was because of how horrible his wife was. He announced to me that he was going to divorce her. I asked the usual question, "Has she been unfaithful to you?" He answered, "Well, no, but I'm just not happy."

I heard the word "happy" and in that moment the Holy Spirit put a thought into my heart and mind. I said, "Oh, you thought you had the right to be happy? There is the problem." I continued, "You see, the government of the United States tells us that we have the right to life, liberty, and the pursuit of happiness. The Declaration of Independence is indeed a marvelous document that acknowledges rights to people who live in the United States. Probably the most influential and well-crafted line from any document of the Founding Fathers is found in the Declaration. It says, "We hold these truths to be self-evident, that all men are created equal, that they are endowed by their Creator with certain unalienable Rights, that among these are Life, Liberty and the pursuit of Happiness." While that is a very gracious thing for our government to try to promise, when it comes to happiness, the Bible guarantees us no such right."

It *is* true that all men are created equal, and it *is* true that we are given rights by our Creator. Life is a right. Liberty or freedom is a right, but I have to question happiness as a right. There are thousands of promises in the Bible, but I have never found one that promises happiness. (I am not saying that God wants us unhappy, simply that there is no promise for it. Jesus did say, "that my joy may be in you and that your joy may be complete" (John 15:11). There is a big difference between happiness and joy. Happiness is dependent on circumstances. We can have joy—independent of our circumstances.) Not only do we not find such a promise but, to the contrary, in Psalm 10 we read, "The wicked man . . . says to himself, 'Nothing will shake me; I'll always be happy and never have trouble.'"

At the end of the book of Jonah, the former fish-bait prophet is sitting on a hill watching Nineveh to see whether or not the city will be destroyed by God. While he sat there God provided a vine that grew very rapidly and *provided* shade for Jonah. And we read in Jonah 4:6 that Jonah was *very happy* about the vine. But the next day, God *provided* (same word) a worm. (By the way, it is also the same word used when it says that God *provided* a great fish to swallow Jonah in the ocean.) So, God provides a fish to eat him and this scary worm that can destroy a vine overnight. If all that were not enough, the next day God *provided* (same word) a scorching east wind, and the sun blazed on Jonah's head. Now, instead of being a happy guy, Jonah said, "It would be better for me to die than to live" (Jonah 4:9). Now, what happened? How could he, in one day, go from being a happy guy to so depressed he became suicidal? Here is the answer:

- Because Jonah was focused on himself rather than *others.*
- Because he was focused on himself rather than the *good news* he brought to the people of Nineveh so they could repent and be saved.
- Because his focus was on himself rather than *the Lord*, who was more interested in Jonah becoming who He wanted him to be than in Jonah's happiness. (It wouldn't hurt to read that one again a couple of times.)

I want you to see that three out of four things God provided for Jonah did not make him happy—but they made him better! The problem with happiness is that it depends on circumstances. Jonah was only happy 25 percent of the time. And the problem with our Founding Fathers' statement is, if we pursue happiness, if happiness is our goal, the thing we are striving for, we will find that it is an empty pursuit indeed. If we asked the apostle Paul, "Are you happy that you are in that prison?" he would say, "No but I have joy in the Lord."

If we are striving for happiness we will come up short. However, if we pursue Christ and make Him our focus then we can always have joy. No one and nothing can take that away.

Besides the so-called "right" to happiness, we also think we have a bevy of other rights. Let me try to enumerate some of these "rights" and, as I do, pay attention to your own heart and soul. See if, at any point, you feel a rise in emotion when you hear one or more of these things. It may indicate an area where you need to relinquish a right.

We think we have the right to:
- Have and control personal belongings
- Privacy
- Have and express personal opinions

- Earn and use money
- Plan our own schedules
- Respect
- Have and choose friends
- Belong, be loved, and be accepted
- Be understood
- Be supported
- Make our own decisions
- Determine our own future
- Have good health
- Enjoy entertainment
- Be married
- Have children
- Have a fulfilling sex life
- Be considered worthwhile and important
- Be protected and cared for
- Be appreciated
- Travel
- Have a fulfilling job
- A good education
- Be treated fairly
- Be desired
- Have fun
- Raise children our way
- Security and safety
- Have hopes and aspirations fulfilled
- Be successful
- Have others obey us
- Have our own way
- Be free of difficulties and problems
- _____

- _____
- _____

- _____

(Extra lines for additional rights you wish to add.)

Let me ask you something about these perceived rights, hopefully without being too grotesque. Does a corpse worry about any of these things? Does a dead man get upset because he is not experiencing these rights? Now, remember where this all started. "I have been crucified with Christ. I no longer live." Can a dead man be insulted or hurt in any way?

I came across the following news article one day:

> Ricky D. Larson was found shot to death near the city limits of La Crosse, Wisconsin. And that's just the problem: Local law enforcement officials aren't sure if he was shot in the city limits, or across the border in the town of Onalaska. It makes a difference since the former is the district of the city police, and the latter would be the responsibility of the county sheriff. Neither agency is particularly eager to pay the costs of the murder investigation. Surveyors are being brought in to see exactly where the city limits are.

I mean how insulting can you get? Nobody cares enough about poor Ricky to take any responsibility to find his murderer. These agencies would rather pay the cost of the surveyor than eagerly seek out justice for this dead man. But does Ricky care that this is going on? Is he concerned that nobody seems to care about him? Is he troubled that his rights to life or dignity have been violated? No! He's dead!

Since we are crucified with Christ we are now also dead and because we are, we have no more rights. Understanding this will really free us up in life. You see, bad things can't hurt us because we're already dead, and when anything good does happen to come our way, we will rejoice because we have no right to have anything. We see that it is the goodness and grace of God that brings good things our way.

A bank in Binghamton, New York, had some flowers sent to a competitor who had recently moved into a new building. There was a mix-up at the flower shop, and the card sent with the arrangement read, "With our deepest sympathy." The florist, who was greatly embarrassed, apologized. But he was even more embarrassed when he realized that the card intended for the bank was attached to a floral arrangement sent to a funeral home in honor of a deceased person. That card read, "Congratulations on your new location!"

When we die physically, we go to a new location. When we come to Christ, we die spiritually and go to a new location. So, congratulation on your new location! Let me tell you about it.

Christ Lives in Me

Now that I've got everybody dead with no rights anymore, let me share that this is not the end of the story. It is only half of it. Yes, I am crucified with Christ. And, true, I no longer live. The flame of my old life is extinguished, but something new has happened: "Christ lives in me!" Thank God! I'm not dead after all. I'm really alive, but I'm not the "me" I used to be.

Say this aloud: "I'm not the 'me' I used to be."

Colossians 3:1–3 reiterates this very clearly. "Since, then, you have been raised with Christ, set your hearts on things above, where Christ is seated at the right hand of God. Set your minds on things above, not on earthly things. For you died, and your life is now hidden with Christ in God."

This is the beautiful thing that baptism in water symbolizes: the death of the old and the raising to life of the new. I no longer live a self-centered life but a Christ-centered one. Wuest says, "The new life is a Person within a person, living out His

160

life in that person . . . Instead of a sinner with a totally depraved nature attempting to find acceptance with God by attempted obedience to a set of outward laws, it is now the saint living his life on a new principle, that of the indwelling Holy Spirit manifesting . . . the Lord Jesus (in us)."[17]

When we describe what happens when a person comes to salvation in Christ, we tend to use the words "became a Christian." But in the New Testament and early church, the word "Christian" was primarily used by other people who described what they saw believers act like: "They act like Christ." One phrase that Jesus used to describe salvation was, "born again." This is what we really are because the old "us" died and the new "us" was born. This is the teaching of what being saved means in the New Testament. Paul writes, "We always carry around in our body the death of Jesus, so that the life of Jesus may also be revealed in our body. For we who are alive are always being given over to death for Jesus' sake, so that his life may be revealed in our mortal body" (2 Corinthians 4:10–11).

In the chapter on Faith-Full Families, I asked, "Are you *who* you want to be?" Notice I'm not saying are you happy, are you fulfilled, or are you experiencing life like you thought you would? You see, life may deal us a bad hand. The story of my early life's difficulties is mild compared to some of the things others have faced. But the answer for all of us is the same. No amount of persecution, trials, difficulties, or anything else can destroy *who* we are if Christ lives in us.

Since it is true that I no longer live and since it is also true that Christ lives in me, then nothing done to this body or this life I am living can change the "me" God made me to be. I am dead and now Christ lives in me. It sounds good on paper, now how do we do it? I mean, how do we really live this out? The answer is right there in the verse.

I Live by Faith—Transforming Faith

The answer to how Christ lives in me is found in the next

phrase of the verse; "*I live by faith* (emphasis mine) in the Son of God, who loved me and gave himself for me" (Galatians 2:20).

Faith = Believing

Believing is something we do that does not change based on circumstances either good or bad. Believing goes to the core of who we are. "Therefore we are always confident and know that as long as we are at home in the body we are away from the Lord. We live by faith, not by sight . . . So we make it our goal to please him" (2 Corinthians 5:6–9). When I was born again on August 18, 1973, I passed from death to life. My position in Christ is one of life—I am alive in Him. However, my experience or my performance has not always been what it should be.

In other words, I have known Christ for over forty years now and still I blow it. I sin. I don't want to, and yet I do. The Bible says, "I died," but every day is like the "night of the living dead." My flesh—my old man—gets into zombie mode and starts walking around again. It is so frustrating. I still keep clinging to the old life and the rights I thought I had. It is irritating as well because I find that with every compromise I make, there is a cost. How can I change? How can I *become what I truly am*? There is only one way: It is through *transforming faith*.

We are transformed two ways. The first is by the renewing of our minds—primarily through the Word. The second is through worship. As I was reading during my devotions some time ago, a text came alive to me.

> As for me, God forbid that I should boast about anything except the cross of our Lord Jesus Christ. Because of that cross, my interest in this world died long ago, and the world's interest in me is also long dead. It doesn't make any difference now whether we have been

circumcised or not. What counts is whether we really have been changed into new and different people. May God's mercy and peace be upon all those who live by this principle. They are the new people of God. (Galatians 6:14–16 NLT)

That phrase from verse 15 lit up like a neon sign for me. Let me repeat it: "What counts is whether we really have been changed into new and different people." This is transforming faith! Sir Isaac Newton's first law of motion is: Everything continues in a state of rest unless it is compelled to change by forces impressed upon it. In other words, if you don't mess with something it will remain as it is. Unfortunately, this is true of human beings as well. If nothing happens to press us to change, we will remain as we are. What do we think about that? Are we content with the way we are? I for one am discontent with my propensity to go into zombie mode. I want more! Yet in the past, I have said things like, "That's the way I was raised" or "This is just my personality." When we say these things, we are really just making excuses for our behavior and resisting change. We have a choice about our lives. How are we going to live?

Earlier I asked, "Are you who you want to be?" A better question for us all is, "Are we who God made us to be?" None of us has quite arrived yet, but there is a way to work on it. We need transformation!

Transformation is becoming outwardly what we already are on the inside. This is the definition of metamorphosis. When the caterpillar goes into the cocoon, it does not genetically change. He becomes (transforms into) what it always was on the inside. We've been given a new spiritual genetic code—the Christ code: "Christ in us, the hope of glory." We need to be turned inside out, so to speak, so that the Christ in us is seen. The answer is already inside us.

> And we all, who with unveiled faces contemplate the Lord's glory, are being transformed into his image with ever-increasing glory, which comes from the Lord, who is the Spirit. (2 Corinthians 3:18)

As we read and study the Bible and as we draw closer to Him in worship, we encounter Him face-to-face, in a sense, as Moses did—with an unveiled face. In such an encounter, someone is going to change, and it is not going to be the unchangeable God. So to effectively be transformed takes a spiritual act of worship, and we see that we are changing into His likeness. The old "us" died. The new "us" is looking more and more like Jesus every day. The point is: As a believer, the change comes from the inside because that is where Christ is. Trying to change our outward behavior will only frustrate us. Been there—done that! It is a useless pursuit. Outward behavior will change but only as we allow the life of Christ to be lived through us. When we feel our flesh entering into zombie mode, it is time to worship, it is time to be in the Word, it is time to allow the life of Christ to overcome those temptations and inclinations of the flesh. Knowing where the change comes from (inside) is freeing.

When we've been working on a file and try to exit the program, the computer asks, "Do you want to save the changes?" God is working on us—writing to the file of our hearts. But the choice is up to us. We have to make the decision. He doesn't just want us to have faith, He wants us to live by faith. If we feel like God is changing us in some way, even after reading this chapter, do we want to save the changes? Imagine God's pleasure as His children begin to understand what it means to live by faith—being changed more into His image every day.

Chapter Thirteen
Built Up in Faith

What is it about seeing a mountain that causes us to pause and drink in the majesty of it? Recently I traveled with my wife through Glacier National Park, and we couldn't help stopping and commenting at every new vista. It almost seems there is an innate drive within to not only see the summit but to go there. I know that is true for me. When I was younger, I climbed a few mountains that were all less than ten thousand feet, and it was exhilarating. One day a friend suggested we should go to Mount Whitney in California. At 14,505 feet it has the distinction of being the tallest mountain in the all the United States except for Alaska.

I was thrilled at the prospect of going, and we began to make our plans. We would take two days to reach the summit, so there would be a lot of equipment to carry. Tent, sleeping bag and pad, cooking utensils, food, water, video camera, clothing, and more all had to fit into my backpack. I had to be able to carry it several miles uphill. We began our climb, and, from the beginning, the views were incredible. On the morning of the second day when we reached the summit, there was nothing comparable. To stand on the very highest point, knowing we had worked so hard and achieved our goal, was exhilarating.

Mount Whitney may sound impressive to some, but, honestly, it was just a very long hike uphill at high altitude. There was no technical climbing involved; no ropes, harnesses, carabineers, etc. Even so, it was something I had to train for. Before we left I climbed "The Ridge" near our house a few times a week. I pushed myself to go as fast and as hard as I could so that I would be ready for the hike. This is the way it is with anything a person wants to do that is physically challenging. The muscles must be built up so the goal can be achieved.

Exercise Faith

I believe there is a sense in which we can exercise our faith and cause it to grow. We are not talking about climbing mountains but moving them. It is foolish for us to think we can move mountains with little faith. Remember, what Jesus really said was, "If you have faith *as* a mustard seed you will say to this mountain . . ." It is a growing, maturing, building up kind of faith that gets the job done. To reach our goal, we have to get in shape and be built up. We have to spiritually exercise our faith, and so far in this book we have suggested ways to exercise faith in areas of finances, family, tomorrow, healing, direction, rest, and more. We have discussed how speaking the word of faith in a situation will cause growth as well, but I want to address a way which we are told will build us up in faith perhaps like no other. It is like the P90X® or Insanity® Workout for faith.

In Jude verse 20 we read, "But you, beloved, building yourselves up on your most holy faith, praying in the Holy Spirit" (NKJV). Here we see that praying in the Holy Spirit will build our faith. This is what we are after! We want to have faith that is growing stronger and stronger, and Jude explains that one method is to pray in the Holy Spirit.

What is praying in the Holy Spirit? Some would suggest that it simply means Spirit-led prayers or praying in the realm of the Spirit somehow. While these explanations may have some merit, they are not the primary meaning of Jude's words. We know this because we see a similar phrase used in 1 Corinthians 14, where Paul clearly contrasts prayers in languages we understand to those we don't—praying with my mind versus *praying with my spirit*. One is understood by the speaker, the other is not.

> For if I pray in a tongue, my spirit prays, but my mind is unfruitful. So what shall I do? I will pray with my spirit, but I will also pray with my understanding; I will sing with my spirit, but I will also sing with my understanding. (1 Corinthians 14:14–15)

The word "tongue" or "tongues" here in chapter 14 is the Greek word used for language(s), but this context speaks of languages that are unknown. There are known languages, and there are unknown ones as well. In 1 Corinthians 13:1 Paul said, "If I speak in the tongues (languages) of men and of angels." Paul seems insistent that a person should pray in his known language as well as a spiritual language. Again he says, "If I pray in a tongue (language) my spirit prays, but my mind is unfruitful." In other words, he cannot understand what he is praying. Does this lack of understanding mean it is of no or little value? Not at all! In fact, it seems that he places equal in value to praying in words he knows and praying in the Spirit in words he does not know by saying he will pray both ways and sing in both as well.

I can hear someone objecting, *Didn't Paul say, "I would rather speak five intelligible words to instruct others than ten thousand words in a tongue"* (1 Corinthians 14:19)? Indeed he did say that, but the previous four words in the verse qualify that particular sentence. He said, "But in the church . . ." *In the church* he would rather be understood, but in his own devotional prayer life he is saying—actually bragging it seems—"I thank God that I speak in tongues more than all of you" (1 Corinthians 14:18). Looking back at verse 5 of chapter 14 we see that Paul seems to be emphasizing prophecy over tongues in the church. However, we see him also say, "Unless he interprets." The word "unless" is like an equal sign. Prophecy = Tongues and Interpretation. All of this is in the context of the local church.

It is not a condemnation of speaking in tongues (languages) that are unknown, and in no way does it demean the private, devotional use of a prayer language. In fact, look at all the positive things Paul says about praying in the Spirit or praying in unknown languages. Below are excerpts from 1 Corinthians 14 in which I have emphasized the high regard Paul has for these unknown languages in both the church and the life of the individual.

- For anyone who speaks in a tongue *does not speak to people but to God*. Indeed, *no one understands* them; they *utter mysteries* with their spirit.
- Anyone who speaks in a tongue *edifies themselves*, but the one who prophesies edifies the church.
- *I would like every one of you to speak in tongues*, but I would rather have you prophesy. The one who prophesies is greater than one who speaks in tongues, *unless someone interprets, so that the church may be edified*.
- For if I pray in a tongue, *my spirit prays*, but my mind is unfruitful.
- So what shall I do? *I will pray with my spirit*, but I will also pray with my understanding; *I will sing with my spirit*, but I will also sing with my understanding.
- *Tongues*, then, *are a sign*, not for believers but *for unbelievers*; prophecy, however, is not for unbelievers but for believers.
- What then shall we say, brothers and sisters? When you come together, *each of you has* a hymn, or a word of instruction, a revelation, *a tongue* or an interpretation. Everything *must be done* so that the church may be built up.
- Therefore, my brothers and sisters, be eager to prophesy, and *do not forbid speaking in tongues*.

According to Jude and Paul, we are individually built up or edified by praying in unknown languages. Additionally, we see that the Church is also built up when unknown languages are accompanied by interpretation.

> Now I want you all to speak in tongues, but even more to prophesy. The one who prophesies is greater than the one who speaks in tongues, unless someone interprets, so that the church may be built up. (1 Corinthians 14:5 ESV)

Praying in the spirit is a power boost to our faith. Here is one reason why: When we trust God enough to believe that what sounds like foolishness coming from our mouths is a heavenly language, we are exercising faith. We like the idea of some of the other gifts mentioned in 1 Corinthians 12: wisdom, knowledge, faith, healing, miraculous powers, prophesy, distinguishing between spirits. These all seem so much more mature and interesting than tongues. I believe this is precisely why tongues seems to be first. It was prominent on the Day of Pentecost for sure, and it seems to be throughout the book of Acts when people are baptized in the Holy Spirit as a sign of this baptism.

Let the River Flow

In John 7, Jesus attends a feast with His disciples. The feast mentioned is the Feast of Tabernacles. It was a weeklong celebration festival, which was a memorial of the time when Israel lived in tents during their wilderness wanderings. Exodus 23:16 indicates that it was also a Feast of Ingathering, one of the three feasts that all male Jews were required to attend annually (see also Deuteronomy 16:16). This particular feast mentioned here in John was about six months before the Passover on which Jesus would die on the cross. He is nearing the end of His ministry. With that in mind, on this greatest day of the feast, Jesus stood up and called out. This is an incredibly important announcement, and He doesn't want anyone to miss it.

> "Let anyone who is thirsty come to me and drink. Whoever believes in me, as Scripture has said, rivers of living water will flow from within them." (John 7:37–38)

Here Jesus has spoken something very profound. Unfortunately, the people who were there at that time immediately started arguing about whether or not He was the Christ and that the Christ could not come from Galilee. Thank God, somebody was listening to what He said and later wrote it down for us. We can read through a couple of verses like that and not really give it much thought, but I believe the Lord had a reason for lifting His voice and making this pronouncement.

His invitation is *not* to just anyone. It is an invitation for those who are *thirsty*. The word for thirst means "the state resulting from not having drunk anything for a period of time." It means to eagerly long for something. Have you ever been really thirsty? Or really hungry? Or have you ever had a passion for something so much that you couldn't think straight? This is the kind of thirst Jesus is talking about. For those who are that thirsty, the invitation is to come and drink, and the result will be "streams of living water will flow from within."

The King James Version says, "out of his belly shall flow rivers of living water." In some cultures the "stomach" is often considered the seat of emotions, but for English speakers the "heart" symbolically has that function. In reality, belly or heart are just ways of saying that there is more to us than a collection of organs—somehow we can feel things deep inside us. People sometimes use the expression, "I had a gut feeling." Where does this part of who we are come from except that we are created in God's image and have a spirit side that can feel and be moved and sense things?

Jesus is saying that it is this part of us, our inmost being—not a literal belly but who we really are apart from our bodies—this part now touched by the work of the Holy Spirit is to be a source of life flowing to the world around us. To come to the place where out of us flows "streams of living water" we have to start by drinking deeply of the Lord. Jesus speaks of this thirst being satisfied, and then He goes on to explain what He means exactly. Don't miss this . . .

> By this He meant *the Spirit* (emphasis mine), whom those who believed in him were later to receive. Up to that time the Spirit had not been given, since Jesus had not yet been glorified. (John 7:39)

Be Baptized with the Spirit

On the day Jesus rose from the dead, He appeared to His disciples. John 20:22 describes Him breathing on the disciples and saying, "Receive the Holy Spirit." I feel confident in saying that if the resurrected Christ stands before you, breathes on you, and says, "Receive the Holy Spirit," you will definitely *receive* the Holy Spirit. But less than forty days later Jesus will say to these same disciples, "Wait for the gift my Father promised, which you have heard me speak about. For John baptized with water, but in a few days you will be baptized with the Holy Spirit" (Acts 1:4–5).

Clearly these disciples had received the Holy Spirit on Resurrection evening, but they had not received the gift the Father had promised, which is the baptism of the Holy Spirit. The disciples did not have all that they needed on the day of His resurrection or even on the day of His ascension. There was more that Christ intended them to receive. Even today, many people willingly ask Christ to come be their Savior and, with that, receive the Holy Spirit inside them, but they have not received the gift—the baptism of the Spirit—where the Holy Spirit comes upon them in power. Salvation and the baptism of the Holy Spirit are not the same thing.

Back to John 7:39. Read this verse again, "By this (the streams of living water flowing) He meant the Spirit, whom those who believed in him were later to receive. Up to that time the Spirit had not been given, since Jesus had not yet been glorified." The words "Jesus had not yet been glorified" speak of a process that began with the Crucifixion, led to the Resurrection, and culminated in the Ascension. Until He ascended and sent His Holy Spirit, no one could receive this baptism. It was on the fortieth day after the Resurrection that Christ ascended and was glorified. It was ten days later, on the day of Pentecost, that this baptism of the Holy Spirit was poured out on the waiting, willing, and thirsty disciples.

So, when we "receive the Holy Spirit" in the context of John 7:39, we are not talking about becoming a believer and the Spirit taking up residence inside us, but we are talking about a baptism of fire that comes upon people who are already believers. It is those who have received this power who are described as people from whom streams of living water would flow. It is this baptism of the Spirit that has been the primary factor in revival and awakening throughout the earth from the early church until now.

Live a Holy Life

You know, I really miss the old days of legalism. (Please notice my tongue in my cheek.) I mean I know legalism is wrong, but at least when people became Christians they knew it was supposed to result in a radically different lifestyle than the way the world lived. When I got saved, I was told that Christians didn't drink or dance or listen to rock 'n' roll music. It was great because you knew who the other believers were.

Currently this mushy and misunderstood environment we live in seems to imply that becoming a Christian is more like deciding to be a member of Costco or choosing a political party. We hear people say, "I'm saved by grace." But often what they mean by that is grace has somehow become an excuse to be worldly, to live pretty much however they want.

My thinking is that if we are saved by grace and living like hell then we don't know at all what grace really is. Look at this verse from 2 Timothy 1:9, "[God] has saved us and called us to a holy life—not because of anything we have done but because of his own purpose and grace."

Did you see that? God called us to live a holy life *because of His grace!* I'm talking about holy living like in the New Testament and in the time of the Great Awakenings in America and other revivals of the past. Of course, the answer is not legalism (tongue is now removed from cheek). Legalism is the law, and the law is useless for changing behavior because ultimately we will do what our flesh dictates. God's Law is perfect, but it proves our inability to keep it. The answer is not a misunderstood form of grace that becomes an excuse for our bad behavior. It is not *saying* we are Christians but we are not really changed and we don't live the holy lives God wants us to. The answer is Spirit fullness—Spirit baptism! The baptism of the Spirit should result in a radically different behavior and lifestyle that flows from within our innermost being (like a river) not from an external set of rules made by men. Look at Paul's reasoning on the matter in these three passages.

> For what the law could not do in that it was weak through the flesh, God did by sending His own Son... that the righteous requirement of the law might be fulfilled in us who do not walk according to the flesh but according to the Spirit. (Romans 8:3–4 NKJV)

> Now the works of the flesh are evident, which are: adultery, fornication, uncleanness, lewdness, idolatry, sorcery, hatred, contentions, jealousies, outbursts of wrath, selfish ambitions, dissensions, heresies, envy, murders, drunkenness, revelries, and the like;

of which I tell you beforehand, just as I also told you in time past, that those who practice such things will not inherit the kingdom of God. (Galatians 5:19–21 NKJV)

But the Holy Spirit produces this kind of fruit in our lives: love, joy, peace, patience, kindness, goodness, faithfulness, gentleness, and self-control. There is no law against these things! (Galatians 5:22–23 NLT)

The picture of fruit here in Galatians is perfect because fruit trees don't have to work at producing fruit. In us, the fruit of the Holy Spirit is produced naturally because it comes from within. Everybody needs the baptism of the Holy Spirit for the power of this kind of release to happen. Jesus said, "But you will receive power when the Holy Spirit comes on you; and you will be my witnesses . . ." (Acts 1:8). I have heard many preachers, myself included in the past, misquote this verse to say, "You will receive power to be witnesses." Now certainly the power of the baptism of the Spirit will aid us in many areas of life, including our ability to witness to others but Jesus actually said, "But you will receive power when the Holy Spirit comes on you; *and* (emphasis mine) you will be my witnesses." "And" is a tiny word, and it is easy to miss it, but Jesus said it. Just to make sure, I checked the Greek text and it belongs there. My point is this: The power He promised is for more than being a witness. It has implication for miracles and spiritual gifts, but perhaps most essential is the power to live a holy life for God. (Thank you to Dr. Steve Schell for helping me see this.)

People may hear this and think, *I want that kind of power working in my life. I want the baptism of the Holy Spirit, but do I have to speak in tongues?* Unfortunately we have focused so much on tongues that it has become a distraction. People who are baptized in the Holy Spirit can and should (at least Paul wishes they would) speak in these unknown languages, but tongues is not the baptism. The baptism is a river flowing with living water; it is a tree bearing good fruit; it is the receiving of power in our lives that results in changed behavior and effective witness throughout the world.

Have you received the baptism of the Holy Spirit? If you have not, what is stopping you? Ask for and receive the baptism by faith. You will know when you have received.

If we have received the baptism of the Spirit, are we allowing the river to flow? Are we becoming more holy in our lifestyle? It takes faith to receive the baptism of the Holy Spirit, and it takes faith to speak in unknown languages, but praying in those languages will build up our faith. Those who are strong in faith are the mountain movers.

Look with me into the distance. Do you see that mountain we need to move? We will have to get in shape for this. Our faith will need to be increased, but we can do it. Let's get into training now. Let's get built up in our most holy faith so we can do more of what is pleasing to God.

Chapter Fourteen
Saved by Faith

In chapter 10 we looked at the story of a man whose life was turned upside down one night. One moment he was about to kill himself, and in the next he realized he had something to live for. It was in that moment he asked Paul the apostle, "What must I do to be saved?" and Paul replied, "Believe in the Lord Jesus, and you will be saved."

It is simple, straightforward, and the same for everyone: To be saved we must believe or have faith in the Lord Jesus. Some might ask, *What do I need to be saved from?* According to the Bible, every human being needs to be saved from their sins and ultimately from eternal death. Someone may object and say it is wrong to judge someone else, but we need to understand that it is not humans judging one another. Instead, it is God judging all humans. According to Him, everyone has sinned and even one sin is enough to separate us from Him. By definition, separation from God ultimately means eternal death. But God presents us with a solution to this dilemma. He sent His own Son to planet Earth to die for our sins. In fact, the Bible tells us that the judgment we should have received for our sins came upon Jesus instead. The day Jesus was crucified was the saddest and most horrible day in all history.

Thankfully, the story was not over. Jesus was sinless, so death could not keep Him dead and the grave had to release Him. It is the resurrection of Jesus on the third day that turned that horrible day into the greatest day ever. The Bible calls this event *the Good News*. Perhaps the best known verse of the Bible is John 3:16. This is because it contains the most concise description of the way a person can have eternal life. Here is that verse and two that follow. Please take a moment to read this carefully and note the four times the word believe is used in the text.

> For God so loved the world that he gave His one and only Son, that whoever believes in him shall not perish but have eternal life. For God did not send his Son into the world to condemn the world, but to save the world through him. Whoever believes in him is not condemned, but whoever does not believe stands condemned already because they have not believed in the name of God's one and only Son. (John 3:16–18)

The contrast between the person who "believes" and the person who does not is stark—it is life or death. Faith makes the difference.

Through Faith We Are Saved

"What must I do to be saved?" . . . "Believe in the Lord Jesus, and you will be saved." Have faith in Jesus, and you will be saved. The first thing to do with faith is use it to begin a relationship with God. The Bible teaches, "It is by grace you have been saved, through faith" (Ephesians 2:8). Grace is God doing for us what we could not do for ourselves. The way we acquire grace is by believing.

Let me illustrate this further: Picture living on a tropical island, enjoying the warm sun and light breeze. It is wonderful. Suddenly, we hear a rumbling on the island, and we look to see smoke billowing and lava flowing out of the top of the volcano. We hear announced that this volcano is really going to blow and everyone on the island will perish if they do not get off. Some believe this message and some do not. Some think they will just wait it out. Fortunately, we believe the report and hurry to the airport. There a Boeing 747, with enough room for every person on that island, is fueled and ready to go. We are told to hurry and get a ticket so we can leave on the plane. As we go to the counter to buy our ticket, we get out our money, but the Owner of the airline is standing there and He says, "No charge." He is offering free tickets to anyone who believed the report. So we are given a boarding pass and off we go. Just as the jet is taking off and gaining altitude, the volcano blows, and we watch in horror as the lava overcomes the entire island and everyone who *chose to stay* is destroyed.

What I have just described is not much different than what we are experiencing on planet Earth right now. God is the owner of the airline. He also knows everything about the island and knows it will be destroyed. Grace is the 747. Grace will get us from where we are to where we need to be. It is a gift from God that has the ability (among other things) to transport us to eternal life. It is by grace we have been saved. Faith is the boarding pass. Grace by itself will not get us off the island. We must present our boarding pass of faith. The plane is going with or without us. Grace is a gift from God. And the way we appropriate God's grace for salvation is through faith. This is exactly what the Bible teaches about being saved:

> But what does it say? "The word is near you; it is in your mouth and in your heart," that is, the message concerning faith that we proclaim: If you declare with your mouth, "Jesus is Lord," and believe in your heart that God raised him from the dead, you will be saved. For it is with your heart that you believe and are justified, and it is with your mouth that you profess your faith and are saved. (Romans 10:8–10)

The words "believe in your heart" mean to have faith. If we believe, we are given the boarding pass and God's grace will carry us to eternal life. In reality, God does not "send" people to hell. People will go to hell because they rejected the gift of life that was offered. If we just believe the message of God that destruction is coming and that He has eternal life for us, then we have our boarding pass. We use that faith to enter into grace—grace that is powerful and will lift us up out of our troubles in this life and save us in the life to come.

As we think about how to make God happy, there is nothing that pleases Him more the faith that is placed in His Son so we might have eternal life with Him forever. It is the very reason we were created.

Below is a simple prayer that you can pray to give your life to Christ. The prayer itself will not save you. Having faith in the things you will pray is what is needed. By faith we are saved. If you have not already done so and are ready to fully commit your life to Jesus Christ, why don't you pray this prayer out loud.

> *Heavenly Father, Thank You for loving me so much that you sent Your only Son, Jesus Christ, to this planet to die on the cross so my sins could be forgiven. I admit that I have sinned, and I ask for forgiveness. I choose today to repent and turn from my old way of life.*
>
> *Jesus, I believe You are alive, You are risen from the dead, and I boldly proclaim that You are the Lord of my life starting now. I am giving You control of everything I am. Thank You for saving me. I will live for You from this day forward.*

Conclusion
Nothing Will Be Impossible for You

Pleasing God happens when people exercise faith. There is unlimited potential in the ways we can apply faith to every facet of our lives. Faith is how we start a relationship with God and faith is how we continue to keep our passion for Him alive. The Lord has an expectation that our faith will grow stronger and stronger. When we can continue to have faith in spite of the storms of life, circumstances, and troubles we may face, He is delighted. All believers will have countless opportunities to apply faith principles in their lives.

Rather than feeling like the call for faith is some kind of burden, we should see how truly liberating and freeing it is. The benefits of believing are vast and cannot be overstated. Remember what Jesus said—look at it one more time: "If you have faith like a grain of mustard seed, you will say to this mountain, 'Move from here to there,' and it will move, and nothing will be impossible for you" (Matthew 17:20 ESV). Nothing will be impossible for you—nothing!

I imagine you and I are the same. I need some miracles. There are things I need supernatural help with. There are things I want to see happen that only God can do. The call to grow our faith is clear and loud. The prospect of the impossible becoming possible is extraordinary, and making God happy is what I want to do. Will you join me?

Appendix
Amazing Faith from the Epistles

Below is a list of attributes and blessings we find in the writings of the Epistles that come by faith in one sense or another. Many times the writers refer to "the" faith or "your" faith, meaning the concept of salvation and the message of salvation as a whole. When Paul says to Philemon, "I pray that you may be active in sharing your faith," he is talking about sharing the gospel message with others. The following list of verses does not refer to "the" faith or "your/their" faith in that sense but examines what can be obtained through faith. Consider how amazing faith is as we go through much of the New Testament.

- Obedience comes from faith (Romans 1:5)
- We are encouraged by each other's faith (Romans 1:12)
- Righteousness is revealed by faith (Romans 1:17)
- The righteous live by faith (Romans 1:17; Galatians 3:11; Hebrews 10:28)
- God justifies those who have faith in Jesus (Romans 3:26–28, 5:1; Galatians 2:16 3:24)
- Righteousness is credited to us and comes to us by faith (Romans 4:5; Philippians 3:9)
- The promise comes by faith (Romans 4:16)
- We can be strengthened in faith (Romans 4:20)
- We gain access into grace by faith (Romans 5:2)
- Faith comes from hearing the message, and the message is heard through the word of Christ (Romans 10:17)
- We stand by faith (Romans 11:20; 1 Corinthians 1:24)

- God has given each of us a measure of faith (Romans 12:3)
- Our faith is to rest on God's power (1 Corinthians 2:5)
- Faith is given as a manifestation of the Spirit, through the Spirit to some as a special gift (1 Corinthians 12:9)
- Faith without love is nothing (1 Corinthians 13:2)
- We live by faith (2 Corinthians 5:7; Galatians 2:20)
- Those who have faith are blessed (Galatians 3:9)
- By faith we receive the promise of the Spirit (Galatians 3:14)
- The only thing that counts is faith (Galatians 5:6)
- We are saved by faith (Ephesians 2:8)
- Through faith in him we may approach God with freedom and confidence (Ephesians 3:12)
- Christ dwells in our hearts by faith (Ephesians 3:17)
- Faith extinguishes all the flaming arrows of the evil one (Ephesians 6:16)
- We are raised with Christ through faith in the power of God (Colossians 2:12)
- God's work is promoted by faith (1 Timothy 1:4)
- Women will be saved through childbearing if they continue in faith (1 Timothy 2:15)
- Those who have served well gain an excellent standing and great assurance in their faith (1 Timothy 3:13)
- Through faith we inherit what was promised (Hebrews 6:12)
- We can draw near to God in full assurance of faith (Hebrews 10:22)
- By faith we understand that the universe was formed at God's command, so that what is seen was not made out of what was visible (Hebrews 11:3)
- Through faith, kingdoms can be conquered (Hebrews 11:33)

- The testing of our faith develops perseverance (James 1:3)
- We are to be rich in faith to inherit the Kingdom He promised (James 2:5)
- The prayer offered in faith (by the elders of the church) will make the sick person well (James 5:15)
- Through faith we are shielded by God's power (1 Peter 1:5)
- Through faith we receive salvation (1 Peter 1:9)
- Our faith is the victory that overcomes the world (1 John 5:4)

Notes

Introduction
[1] Kenneth S. Wuest, *Wuest's Word Studies from the Greek New Testament* (Grand Rapids: Eerdmans, 1973).

Chapter One
[2] Kenneth S. Wuest, *The New Testament: An Expanded Translation* (Grand Rapids: Eerdmans, 1961).

Chapter Five
[3] Robert Morris, *The Blessed Life: Unlocking the Rewards of Generous Living* (Ventura: Regal, 2004), 22.

Chapter Six
[4] Jerry Cook, *The Monday Morning Church: Out of the Sanctuary and Into the Streets* (New York: Howard, 2006), 86.
[5] I suggest two great books on the subject of healing: 1. *God Still Heals: Answers to Your Questions about Divine Healing* by James L. Garlow & Carol Jane Garlow. 2. *Authority to Heal* by Ken Blue.
[6] *From the Field* (Los Angeles: International Church of the Foursquare Gospel, 2002), 302.

Chapter Eight
[7] Michael Winerip, "Revisiting Y2K: Much Ado About Nothing?" (*New York Times*, May 27, 2013).
[8] Charles Swindoll, Hand *Me Another Brick* (Nashville: Thomas Nelson, 1978), 82–83.
[9] Warren W. Wiersbe, *Wiersbe's Expository Outlines on the New Testament* (Colorado Springs: Cook, 1992).
[10] Thomas O. Chisholm, "Great is Thy Faithfulness" (Carol Stream: Hope Publishing, 1923).

Chapter Nine
[11] *International Standard Bible Encyclopaedia* (Biblesoft Electronic Database, 1996, 2003, 2006).
[12] Philip Yancey, *What's So Amazing about Grace?* (Grand Rapids: Zondervan, 1997), 45.
[13] Lance Witt, *Replenish: Leading From a Healthy Soul* (Ada: Baker, 2011), 18.
[14] Wayne Cordeiro, *Leading On Empty: Refilling your Tank and Renewing your Passion* (Minneapolis: Bethany House, 2010), 34.
[15] Ibid., 34.
[16] Ibid., 23.

Chapter Twelve
[17] Wuest, *Wuest's Word Studies from the Greek New Testament*.

For additional copies please contact the author at:
srdimare@gmail.com

Or through:
Praise Center
www.praisecenteronline.com
509.886.9410